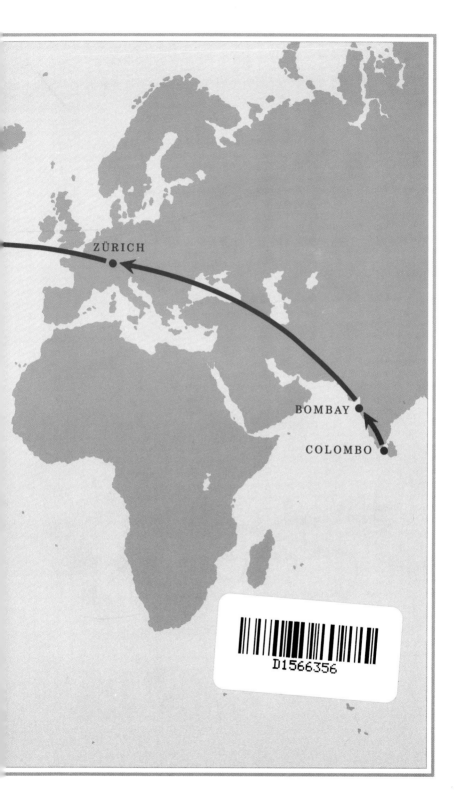

The Long Way Home

Leroy S. Rouner

LANGFORD BOOKS
an imprint of
Diamond Communications, Inc.
South Bend, Indiana

1989

LANGFORD BOOKS
DIAMOND COMMUNICATIONS, INC.
Post Office Box 88
South Bend, Indiana 46624
(219) 287–5008

Library of Congress Cataloging-in-Publication Data

Rouner, Leroy S.
  The long way home.

  1. Bereavement – Religious aspects – Christianity.
2. Theodicy. 3. Mountaineering – Alaska – Accidents
and injuries. 4. Rouner, Leroy S. 5. Rouner,
Timothy Nichols, 1958–1977. 6. Rouner family.
I. Title.
BV4907.R66 1989   155.9′37   89–23363
ISBN 0–912083–40–9

For Rita and Rains; but especially
For Jonathan and Christina,
Who didn't get to come to Alaska

Grief goes with our days – and perhaps is a
holy link with such horrors in the world
as might find us otherwise hard of heart.

Daniel Berrigan

I

Colombo to Bombay,
Wednesday, August 17th, 1977

"Today, I am going home."

That was my first thought as I woke up.

I was lying kitty-corner on the too-short bed which Bubsy Arulampalam and his wife had given up so that I could be comfortable. It was 6:30 A.M. The table fan, which they had also given up, was droning faithfully, keeping the room bearable, but it was already hot. I rolled over to mottled sunshine filtering through the leaves of the jackfruit tree outside my window. A few blocks away diesel buses and lorries were already belching and roaring along a crowded main street in downtown Colombo, and horns were honking furiously, but Fussels Lane, where I was staying, was relatively quiet. A few children at play shouted to each other. There was a regular slapping of wet clothes on flat rock as women did their washing. A street vendor, holding a large basket on his head with one hand and walking purposefully,

3

was crying his wares: "korlee mootaay, korlee mootaay."
I recognized the Tamil for "chicken eggs" and was pleased
with myself for remembering.

I had gone to India in 1961 with my wife, three small
children, a brand new Ph.D., and very little sense of
what I was doing. I knew nothing about India. Except
for a year in a British public school before college, I was
a provincial New Englander, the son of a Congregational
minister in Portsmouth, New Hampshire, who went to
prep school in Connecticut, college in Boston, and graduate school in New York. I had been to Colorado with my
father for the summer when I was thirteen and we went
by train, so I had a feel for the vastness of America's
prairies and the grandeur of the Rockies, but that was
pretty much it. I had never been south and I had never
been to California.

My maternal grandmother had been a missionary in
Burma and Japan, however, and our house in Portsmouth
had oriental carpets and oriental artifacts, including an
ivory statue of the Buddha, with much of the original
gold leaf worn off. So I grew up with the Orient as an
undiscovered part of my world and going to India was
partly claiming my past. It was an odd decision even
so. I had met only a few Indians and didn't like any of
them. My identity was shaped by New England and
the dramatic changes of New England's seasons. And
I was ambitious about advancement in an American
university. So here was a preacher's kid from Portsmouth,
with a passionate feel for New England's seasons, hoping for academic success, going off to the academic back-
waters of South Asia, where they don't have any seasons to speak of.

I wanted to do something good, something sacrificial.
I wanted to be pure in heart. "Be ye therefore perfect,
as your Father in Heaven is perfect" – that was what I

needed to be. So Victorian romanticism and Puritan perfectionism joined hands in my missionary calling. And what could charge the spirit more than an adventure on the other side of the world?

I am a sunlight person. I love clear, bright shining. India is a sunlight place. Immediately I loved the jacaranda trees in bloom, the brilliant hues of women's saris on the streets, and blood-red sunsets over the dusty Indian plains. I learned to love India's warm, soft, dark; the faint, far-off loudspeaker chants of muezzins calling the Muslim faithful to prayer as I worked in my study before dawn; the clinking together of metal tabs on wooden ox-cart wheels at night; the breathy hoot of steam engine whistles at 2:00 A.M., trying unsuccessfully to be shrill. I loved the smell of dust, and the fragrance of cow dung fires.

Cow dung fires and dust is what did it.

I had seen dead bodies in Calcutta. I knew about the drought-starved, monsoon-drowned victims of India's destiny for natural disaster, and I felt the frustrated American instinct for daddying the world's suffering children and making it all right for them; but the smell of cow dung fires and dust was now as much a part of me as the seasonal drama of New England. Perhaps I was there for some wrong reasons, but I was in the right place. At least for a time.

By the end of our five-year term in India I had developed kidney stones, and education for the children had become a problem. We went home for a year's furlough, intending to return, but Rita, my wife, didn't want to because of the children. I was desperate to go back. She and I fought over our future for that whole year, but we finally settled in Boston. I went back to India often to lecture, however, and in the seventies

Bubsy Arulampalam and several other former students of mine in India came to Boston University to do Ph.D.'s.

My visit with Bubsy and his family in Colombo was the last stop on a lecture tour of some five weeks which had taken me to Delhi, Srinagar, Calcutta, Bangalore, and Madurai. Because it was a return to India, I had longed for it in anticipation, and loved the travel and people while I was there. But I had been away for five weeks. I was lonely. I wanted to get home. And I was anxious about Stephen and Timmy's climbing expedition.

They were to meet their friend Peter Cole for a first ascent of the northwest face of Devil's Thumb, outside Petersburg, Alaska, a peak which dominates the landscape at the end of the Baird Glacier. Stephen had been on expeditions of this sort before with Peter, an experienced climber, but this was Timmy's first big expedition. Tim had done a lot of rock and ice climbing when he and Stephen had been at the White Mountain School in Littleton, New Hampshire. Stephen had climbed the North American Dawn Wall and the Nose of El Cap in Yosemite, both major rock climbing adventures, and together he and Tim had done a number of new ice climbing routes in the East. Just a few months earlier Tim and a classmate from Hampshire College had done the Salathe Wall in Yosemite, in the rain.

That, as the climbers say, was an epic.

Rock is slippery when wet. Another team on the Salathe had backed off when the rain started, and one of them was killed in the descent. Timmy never said much about that. Climbers take a jaunty attitude toward death. They call it "buying the farm." And a lot of them do it.

I was fascinated with their climbing. During the year before he went to the White Mountain School, Timmy

6

was regularly after me to go climbing with him at Quincy Quarry, a climber's mecca outside Boston. I went a couple of times, but forty-three is a little late to start that sort of thing.

I hate being scared.

I turn off the TV when people get mean, or start getting killed. On several occasions Tim and I planned to go to Quincy, when a blessed rain fell, so we couldn't go, and I said, "Well, we'll do it another time." I loved going skiing with him and was completely happy from start to finish of a skiing day, but the prospect of those few climbing expeditions was a dark cloud.

I remember those climbs vividly, however, and it gave me a feel for why he wanted to do it. Expert or not, climbers are scared to death most of the time. It is their special high. As a result, the mind is wonderfully fixed on the task at hand. I rowed on the crew at Harvard and, in the midst of a boat race, you are totally absorbed in the race. But you are not about to die; it only feels that way. Climbers *are* about to die, so there is a unique metaphysical seriousness about climbing.

My first climb at Quincy was on a short beginner's wall. Timmy was secure at the top and held the end of a rope tied around my waist. He called down encouragement and directions. At first, the hand and foot holds were prominent and the climb was technically easy. Part way up, however, I came to a move I couldn't make.

Tim called down instructions. Twice I tried desperately and couldn't do it. I was frustrated, humiliated, anxious, and angry. ("I'm fifty feet off the ground. Forget up. How the hell do I get down?") I was trembling from the intensity of my two failures. My shirt was wet through. A couple of fingers were scraped and bleeding, and I had banged my shin during my last short fall before Timmy's rope caught me and stopped my pendulum-swing-scraping on the rock till I could find a toe hold again. I wiped my forehead with my left sleeve and blinked away the sting of sweat. Then I gripped the finger-crack holds above my head, and reached my left foot to the small bump in the rock, waist high, which was the only toe hold. Timmy yelled, "Go for it, Leeroy!" just as I made my excruciating, adrenalin-rush lunge upward.

I made it.

I couldn't believe it. I knew I couldn't make it. I had tried twice with everything I had and failed.

I caught my breath, proudly acknowledged Timmy's cheer, glad that the old man had come through for him, pleased with my prowess, faintly mindful that I had stumbled onto something more than athletic macho. It reminded me of my sophomore year at Harvard when the varsity crew had broken a course record on Lake Cayuga at Cornell, and we were rowing back to the boathouse, full of rowdy pizzazz in the flush of victory. When the boat goes that well you can row forever.

A half mile from the boathouse our stroke quickened our lazy victory paddle and exuberantly we raced home. The beat got higher and higher. There was no competition. There was only the flashing of oars and the glint of sun on the water, and eight oarsmen giving their more-than-everything, becoming one crew. We took off from the water, soared over tree tops, screamed into sunlight, floated past stars, hurtled through galaxies, and only then heard the coxswains' "Way enough!" for our last stroke, as the boat skimmed through softly gurgling water, and we leaned panting over stilled oars. Our coach had been watching intently from his launch. As we slid into the dock he picked up his megaphone and said softly, "Wow!"

My successful climbing move had had a flash of that

same ecstasy, and ecstasy must be a crucial part of climbing's appeal. There is the beauty of the mountains, of course; the challenge of the adventure; the camaraderie of two people totally dependent on each other for their lives. But these are all relations outside yourself. Inwardly, ecstasy is total unity.

To have the mind wonderfully fixed; to will one thing; to live the impossible move, which is not from here to there, from now to then, but a limitless, immeasurable event of a self outside itself, lost in the Moment.

Like rowing through sunlight to stars and galaxies beyond. But for climbers, unlike oarsmen, this is a dance with death, and ecstasy flirts with the demonic. If climbing is a religion, as some say, it is Dionysian, and that is dangerous stuff.

The experience at Quincy didn't make me enthusiastic about rock climbing, but it countered the fear somewhat. Our next expedition was a year later on a route called "Thin Air" at Cathedral Ledge in North Conway, New Hampshire, and this time I wasn't scared in anticipation, only when we got there. Quincy is a practice wall. Cathedral Ledge is a real cliff. Granted, "Thin Air" is what novices do. If you're a climber and your new girlfriend is athletic and game, that's the first climb you take her on. Still, it is "exposed." That means you can see straight down.

I was touched by Timmy's affectionate zeal for this mutual venture, but I was *not* his girlfriend. It was, however, a role reversal. He became the father and I was the son.

I remembered times as a small boy when I had gone strange places, like Boston, with my father and trusted him to get me home safely, and now it was that way with Tim. "Our curly-headed, incandescent boy," as Rita once called him, was now the man in charge. This ven-

9

ture was entirely new to me. I had no idea whether it was safe or not, or whether I could really do it, so I just trusted him. Timmy knew how, and Timmy wouldn't bring me here if it wasn't OK, right?

I had a major success on a sideways move which Tim assured me was very difficult and I would probably fall, so he banged in extra protection to make sure I would be all right. The ground seemed like a mile away, but I was less scared about falling than I was about not being able to make the next move. I didn't fall, and when I got to where Tim was waiting at the end of the move I was feeling like a triumphant Old Man of the Mountains. The mood lasted until we started the last "pitch" to the top. Tim skipped up in a couple of minutes, tied the rope around a tree, and then called encouragement to me below.

Most of it went relatively quickly, but the last major move was an overhang. The rock juts out above you, and you have to pull yourself out, up, and over. The up and over made sense. The out seemed insane. Tim told me I could do it. It was like my first back dive when I was five at Ossipee Lake, standing on the end of the diving board and my father saying, "Attaboy, Lee, you can do it. Just bend your knees, arch your back, and push!" Again, I tried a couple of times and fell off each time. There was no way I could get down. I fantasized about cutting the rope and doing a swan dive off into thin air and thinking "the hell with it." Tim said I should try again, so I heaved mightily, he hauled away on the rope, and finally I did make it.

I stood trembling for a moment, awe-struck by the spectacular view, then turned to him for the truth and said, "You pulled me up that last bit, didn't you?" He said, "Leeroy, I'm not strong enough to pull you over that." I thought, "Now he tells me . . ."

On the hike down the back side of the cliff I found myself musing over my personal list of Dumb Sayings by Wise People. My favorite has always been Socrates' saying that "the unexamined life is not worth living," which I still think is one of the dumbest things anybody ever said. Now I decided that the Number One spot should go to George Mallory's non-explanation about climbing a mountain "because it's there." Clearly, there is more to it than that.

And clearly, it is a crazy thing to do. Too many people get killed doing it. And for what? For ecstasy? I had been thinking about that one early spring weekend in 1977, when Timmy and Stephen and I had all been at High Meadow Farm, our home in New Hampshire. They were going off early the next morning to climb with Peter Cole. I had offered them my new Mercedes, which was already known as "Leeroy's Sacred Benz." I loved that car, and Timmy did, too. It became a real bond between us. When he was away at college, he used to write home and say, "Take a spin in the Benz for me, Leeroy," and I would.

He wrote a story about that climbing expedition, called "The Taking of a Joke." They called each other by their middle names, and "Nichols" was always telling his big brother "Rainsford," or "Rains," that he needed to learn how to take a joke. It was true. Rains could be pretty intense. So they took the Benz before dawn, and left the lights on all day by mistake, and came down from the clinb at night to a dead battery, and didn't get home until the next morning. When the car wouldn't start, and Rains had his characteristic guilt/responsibility reaction, Timmy laughed at their plight and said, "Rains, you've got to learn to take a joke."

Meanwhile, I waited for them, knowing that they were always late, knowing also that I didn't offer to get dinner for them *every* night, and that if they could they would call and let me know. But they didn't come, and after 11:00 I went to bed. I was half awake most of the night. I had a day/night dream that they had both been killed in a fall. In the dream I had a phone call:

"Hello, is Mr. Rouner there? Mr. Rouner, this is Sergeant Swift of the New Hampshire State Police. Do you have someone there with you. . . . ?"

Then he told me that the boys were both dead, and I called Rita in Wayland, and we talked about funeral arrangements, and where we would have the service, and where they would be buried. And in the half-dream I remembered an earlier real phone call late one night when Timmy was at the White Mountain School and the voice said,

"Mr. Rouner, this is Doctor Whatever-his-name-was at the Littleton Hospital."

I was terrified and thought, "Oh *shit!*" but I said, "Yes?"

He said, "We have your son Tim here."

Well, at least it sounded like he was alive.

I said, cautiously, "Yes?"

Dr. Whatever said, "He has appendicitis."

I let out my breath and said, "Oh, good!"

I explained hastily that I had been afraid he'd been in a climbing accident. But now, in my half-wakeful dream, it seemed real, and I was very angry.

"You stupid kids! What did you think you were doing? You threw your whole life away, for *what*? For Chrissake, *what did you think you were doing?*"

Toward dawn I must have drifted off because the phone woke me.

"Leeroy? This is Rains. We're here with Peter. Sorry about last night. The Benz had a dead battery, and we had to go into North Conway to get it fixed."

I wish now I had said how I felt, if, in fact, I even knew, in my numbness. What I actually said was, "Thanks for calling, Rains. See you guys at lunch time."

When they first started climbing there was a long article in the *Boston Globe* by a father who had lost his son on a climb in the White Mountains. I posted that article on my office door at Boston University. Now that my sons were climbers, I was vicariously playing the tragic father, half-awed by the heroism of the venture, half-dreading a bad end. I left that article up for a long time. Maybe I thought it would ward off the evil eye. Mostly I was just showing off this new addition to the family mythology. We had a big house in New Hampshire (as well as our big house in Wayland), and handsome, athletic, high-achieving kids. We had lived for five years in exotic India, and then driven a Land Rover overland to Europe, so we came home with tales of snowball fights in the Afghan mountains on the road north from Kabul to Masar-i-Sharif, and of riding camels in the desert of Baluchistan. To our children's friends we were the family they wished they'd had.

We were all larger than life. The kids were good skiers, had lots of friends, won ribbons at horse shows, and graduated with honors from Harvard and Yale. I was proud of that, and the climbing added to the family mystique of these people with a glint of glory on them, who had everything and could do anything. When friends in India expressed concern for our safety during our overland trip, I refused to be worried, and I didn't really think that I would one day be in the position of the father who wrote that article.

But now I know that scene.

They had scattered his son's ashes from the top of Mt. Chocorua in New Hampshire, and I feel like I was there.

13

Everybody gathers in the trail-base parking lot at the appointed time. No one says very much, but people touch each other a lot. Then they start up the trail. The parents go together, bound by their common loss, separated by their different relation to their lost son, burdened by their common guilt. They did not protect him from death, and being a parent means that at least you don't let your children die. The rest of the company are college-age friends of the dead child, most of them climbers themselves. They are lean, attractive, athletic, some with a superficial scruffiness, which is part of their Whole Earth macho.

At the summit they gather on a high boulder overlooking the valley below and the far reach of the White Mountains beyond. The minister, a friend of the family, says a few words, and then the parents speak about how he was just starting to get it together, and how he loved climbing, and nature, and the mountains; and some of his friends talk about how great it was to be with him, and they celebrate his qualities, and mourn his loss.

They are all dressed in jeans and down jackets and hiking boots, the girls with straight long hair and uplifted faces, crying softly, and the guys with hands jammed in their jacket pockets, heads down, occasionally scuffing at something with the toe of a boot, then squinting at the horizon. They seem troubled and faintly impatient.

Then there is a ceremonial scattering of the ashes, with one or two audible sobs as this very small cloud vanishes almost immediately in the cold spring wind. The minister murmurs about "dust to dust" and the kids are moved by it all, and look out at the beauty of the mountains, and remember their friend, but in their heart of hearts, because they are young and ecstasy still holds them, they do not attend to their vulnerability, and they go on climbing.

14

Climbers seldom give it up because of the death of a friend. They give it up because they get too scared, or too old to make the moves, or they get interested in something else. The philosopher Santayana said that philosophies are not disproven, they are abandoned. Climbing is like that, too. But it isn't death that does it. Death just makes them want to go out and do an epic route for dear old Charley; as if Charley cared.

The expedition to Devil's Thumb had been in the back of my mind ever since I left home. Rains had promised to call as soon as they got back to Petersburg, on August 11th, and Rita had my itinerary so I knew she would let me know if anything happened. She had been away at a conference when I left for India, but all the children were home. The two youngest, Jonathan and Christina, were enjoying the summer weekend, but Rains and Timmy were trying to get their act together for the big expedition.

The floor of the playroom in Wayland was their staging area. The display of climbing equipment was, as the kids say, awesome. There were rows of metal pitons to pound into cracks in the rock, and metal carabiners to clip into the pitons to run the rope through. There were hammers and ice axes, and metal crampons for their boots, and thin nylon ropes of several braided colors, and down jackets, and packs, and different kinds of boots, and canteens, and God only knows what all. The hardware made them seem like medieval knights readying for battle. I kidded them about William James' saying that we needed a "moral equivalent for war" and it looked to me like climbing was it.

Rains was always getting absorbed in something like fitting crampons to his boots, and Timmy was going nuts trying to get him organized. Although two years younger,

Timmy was the older brother in some ways, and the need to get organized brought out Timmy's seniority.

It was Saturday, July 16th, 1977, and I was running around trying to get myself organized to leave for London that evening at 8:30. At one point I herded the children out on the front lawn for a picture. Rains and Tina were perched in the apple tree, while Timmy, Jonathan, and I stood below. Everyone is grinning widely except Tim. Maybe his elder brother responsibilities were getting to him.

That afternoon there were lots of shouts back and forth between me and Rains and Tim to help solve mutual problems of organization. Whatever had dampened Tim's ebullience during the afternoon's picture-taking was gone by the time it came for me to leave. He and Rains insisted that they would take me in the Benz, to see me off, so I left a note for Rita and hugged Jonathan and Tina goodbye. We got to Logan Airport well before 8:30. When it came time to go, Rains and Timmy walked me to the gate.

I gave them each a long proud hug and said what I always said before they went climbing: "Be careful; and have a good time." That's the last thing I ever said to Timmy. I went through the metal detector, had my ticket checked, and just before going down the runway, I turned around.

They were standing there saluting me with their arms raised high, already tan from the summer sun, strong and young, full of promise, eager for their great adventure. Timmy had just turned nineteen. I loved them with one last wave, and then got on the plane.

Later, Rita wrote me in India about their departure:

> Now regarding the Alaskan expedition, I am feeling *very* apprehensive about the whole

thing and am wishing we had paid closer attention to what the boys were planning and how they were going about it. I'm afraid that it is turning out to be a very "half-assed" arrangement and that if they get into any kind of serious trouble they will end up having "bought the farm," as Timmy colorfully (and obscurely) puts it. We all know my tendency toward undue anxieties and alarms but focusing on Reet's proverbial hysteria is always a way of avoiding taking a hard look at other elements in the situation, which, when duly examined, don't bear scrutiny. I'm *definitely* unwilling to be used in this way as a diversion any longer!!! It's too late to do anything now except pray (which I've lined up several people at Adelynrood, St. Andrew's, the Convent of St. Margaret's, and various other reliable sources to do between now and Aug. 20th) but another time I hope you will inform yourself of their plans and at least make them consider whether they have planned adequately for possible emergencies. I think we should have insisted on some kind of radio contact or some way to maintain touch with other people during the three-week interval that they will be in the wilderness.

Their departure was a scramble as usual but we all had a good time and everyone was very cheerful and cooperative. As soon as you left, New England was hit with a horrendous heat wave lasting for five days, with temperatures in the high 90s and 100s day after day. It was fierce! Jay (Jonathan) was very good-humored and didn't fuss about the mess, which was considerable, since they had their gear spread out all over the place. Stephen spent hours fussing over a pair of crampons and new boots, adjusting them to each other, and Tim seemed to be the one who took responsibility for everything else: food, tickets, travelers checks, camping gear, etc. They made one trip to Sandwich and then discovered that they hadn't looked properly through that trunk under the ping-pong table and so needed to go back to Sandwich for something else. (Help!) It became obvious that they would never make the bus and I wanted to be with them anyway (of course!) so I offered to drive them to Montreal, going by way of Sandwich and North Conway so they could get some other things that they forgot at Eastern Mountain Sports. We had a great ride up, except for the fact that Stephen took so long in North Conway, disappearing for over an hour to track down Rick Willcox and retrieve some old rock-climbing boots, that we were afraid we were going to miss the train. . . .

In Montreal we found the railroad station easily (in plenty of time as it turned out) and I bade them a fond farewell as they trundled off like laden pack mules to the train.

When I got back to the car I found an ice hammer in the trunk under a down hood . . . I had been feeling jubilant at their exuberance and general dear-ness until I found the hammer, which I'm *sure* they did not mean to leave. At that moment I became very alarmed and anxious and have been so ever since.

18

While Rita had been helping the boys get ready for Montreal, I had been visiting friends in England, negotiating with publishers in the Hague, and then spending a few days with my sister and her husband, who lived in Munich. My mother and father were also there on a visit, and I had an important conversation with my father. He told me details of his childhood which I had not known before.

He was then in his eighties, about six feet tall, handsome with a large, square head, deep-set eyes, large nose and expressive mouth, and a full head of white hair. His muscular body was now stout, but erect. He laughed easily and often. Humor did not graze him lightly; it stormed through him and blew him away. The helplessness of his laughter was an endearing vulnerability in a man whose bearing was rather formal and whose convictions were dogmatic.

Everyone liked him. Several men said to me, "Your father is the nicest fellow I ever met." He made friends wherever he went. Having come from humble origins, he was too much impressed with people in high places, or of great repute; but the people he liked most were ordinary folk like himself, who had warm hearts and generous spirits. He and my mother once had car trouble on a trip through Texas and the service manager at the garage, one Del Crow, was very good to them during the several days it took to fix the car. They kept in touch with the Crows for the twenty years until Mother and Dad died, even though I don't know that they ever saw them again. That was typical.

My father's mother had run away from home as a young girl and was still a teenager when my father was born. He never knew his father, whose name was Harry McFadden, and I'm not sure Harry and my grandmother were ever married. Harry had gone to Colorado to get

19

a job. He returned once when my father was a baby. Dad told me that he remembered crawling under the bed, playing with a pistol – he never explained the pistol – when a man came in the room, argued with his mother, and stormed out.

All Dad ever saw of his father was his shoes.

When, in her eighties, my grandmother lay comatose and dying, she cried out, "Oh Harry! Come and see what a fine boy you have!"

Grandma Rouner, as we children called her, had had only a fourth-grade education, but she was spirited and smart. My father was born and raised in Omaha, Nebraska, around the turn of the century. The family was just him and his mother. She was only about sixteen years older than he was, and he said that they grew up like brother and sister. Their first house had no running water or electricity, and the unpaved road in front of it was often choked with the dust of cattle drives to the stockyards. Later, she made a practice of buying a house, fixing it up, and then selling at a profit, so they moved regularly. Eventually she bought a large house and took in boarders.

Dad was an avid reader of Horatio Alger and Frank Merriwell stories. He had had a regular after-school job ever since he was eight years old, but in the evenings he read by a kerosene lamp and determined to make something of himself. The YMCA helped, and eventually he went to Harvard and Union Seminary in New York and became a distinguished Congregational minister in Portsmouth, New Hampshire, and later in Brooklyn, New York. My brother and I also went to Harvard and Union and became Congregational ministers. My father's influence on us was considerable.

The conversation with Dad in Munich turned to his mother and a fellow named Earl, whom she had maried when Dad was about fifteen. Dad had only recently told us that his mother had shot and killed Earl for running around with other women. I was shocked and secretly thrilled with this revelation. The flow of time had washed away the personal anguish which he and my grandmother had suffered, and I was free to exploit this Wild West story for my own need. I needed freedom from the oppressive goodness of Horatio Alger and his inevitable success. Years later, after my father died, I heard Norman Vincent Peale preach for the first time, and I wished that Dad had been there, because the Power of Positive Thinking was also his gospel. My father was the best decision maker I ever knew. He was always clear about what he wanted and he never looked back.

He did not learn from his mistakes because he could not remember having made an important mistake.

He said he had decided early in life that he believed in the good and didn't believe in evil, and he couldn't be bothered worrying about the bad things that had happened to him. He was surprised to realize he had not told us before about his mother shooting Earl, but that was like him. He was very good at walking away from things. Repressed feelings are supposed to come back to haunt you, but they didn't seem to with him. He didn't have bad dreams, he had empty places.

I had followed in my father's footsteps and been glad for them, and it had worked. He sent all of his children to private prep schools, and I loved Choate, and Harvard, and Union Seminary, and the Congregational ministry. And emulating Horatio Alger is a great way for an ambitious kid to get out of poverty on the wrong side of the stockyards in Omaha, circa 1900; but what if a really bad thing happens that you cannot walk away from?

21

Like my father and Horatio Alger, my life had been full of sunlight and the good. Hard work and zealous morality had paid off. At Choate we scholarship kids worked our butts off to beat the rich bastards from Greenwich and Westchester County, who got convertibles for graduation but who also got kicked out for smoking, or squeaked through with minimal grades. We cultivated quiet scornfulness, the anti-snob snobbery of the morally superior.

We were the honor roll crowd; the three-letters-a-year-in-varsity-sports people; the winners of graduation day prizes for excellence in English, or mathematics, or, best of all, for "having done the most for the School."

That was the big prize, and I won it.

Later, however, the thought of Choate made me strangely restive, as though I had loved it too much. My passion for success was a craving for approval. I was running for President of the World without asking myself whether that was a job I really liked or wanted. I did it for Dad, and Choate, and Good People everywhere. I had become a character in my own Horatio Alger story, which I knew was too good to be true. Why hadn't someone at Choate told me that? Didn't they know? Was their world also full of willful dreamers, like my father, who could shape life to their making, and never have to come to terms with bad things?

So there in Munich Dad and I talked about Grandma Rouner, and Earl, and how Dad had given his mother a pistol for her birthday that year, and when she complained about Earl's dalliances, Dad had bought a false moustache and a bowler hat and trailed Earl on the streetcar to the barroom where he was shacked up with his girlfriend, and Dad told my grandmother, who marched off to the barroom, and confronted Earl. He taunted her and told her to get out. She, in a fit of passion (as they say), whipped out her birthday pistol and with one shot did him in. It was a "Frankie and Johnny" story.

> The sheriff came round in the morning.
> Said it was all for the best.
> He said her loving Johnny
> was nothing but a doggone pest.
> He was her man,
> but he was doing her wrong.

I told this story to anyone who would listen.

I figured that a skeleton in the family closet was just what I needed, and could go a long way toward countering the moral perfectionism of YMCA muscular Christianity, and the inevitably successful optimism of Horatio Alger. I wrote something about this event a few days later. The occasion was a letter to Rita from Calcutta on August 3rd, which turned out to be the day Timmy died. I had been speculating about the intense emphasis on sexual purity in my family upbringing. Why was sexual immorality the seemingly unforgivable sin?

> ... I have been thinking some more about Grandma Rouner shooting that fellow, . . . trying to put myself in Dad's situation when he was fifteen or so and had this thing happen to him. He seems to have forgotten, but his comment that he earned the money to buy his mother a pistol, so that he had "had a hand in it," as he put it, gradually makes me think that, in fact, the whole thing was a terrible trauma for him. . . . He not only bought her the pistol, he showed her the way to go to do the deed.

23

Of course he didn't know that she was going
to shoot the guy, and he says that she says
that everything went blank for her, and it was
indeed a crime of passion, BUT: a) she had it
in for the guy; and b) she owned a pistol and
knew how to use it. And there is Dad, with his
upwardly mobile morality, and yet, at the same
time, his rough and ready semi-frontier background. ("Here, Mother dear, I bought you
this pistol for your birthday, in case any of
these boardinghouse bastards gives you a hard
time, you can shoot them with it.") And his
mother came home from this expedition which
he helped make possible and says that she has
used his birthday pistol to shoot old Earl. . . .

You can't be horrified at Mother, because she
is all you have, and you've got to stick together.
If you are horrified at screwing around, this
both excuses the deed, and justifies your lack
of feeling about old Earl, because justice was
done. "I never liked him anyway, and that's
what you get if you screw around, so Mother
was a little impetuous, but Hell knows no fury
like a woman scorned, and we can all understand that, and there isn't any more to be said
about it so we might as well just forget the
whole thing. I would have told my children
about it when they got old enough, but actually, I just forgot. . . ."

I was still luxuriating in the mottled sunshine filtering through the leaves of the jackfruit tree outside my
window, with the sounds of early morning street life on
Fussels Lane, when the alarm went off. I was booked

on SwissAir Flight 315 from Colombo to Bombay at 10:10 A.M., and 6:30 was none too early to get moving.

I swung my legs over the side of the bed, sat there for a moment rubbing my eyes and getting my bearings before stumbling into the bathroom. I slipped out of my shorts, and stood naked in the middle of a small room containing a toilet, a wash basin, a floor drain in the corner toward which the floor tilted, and a brass water tap on the wall about two feet above the drain. Under the tap was a two-quart aluminum pot with a handle. The floor and walls were red-coated cement. I filled the pot with water, dumped it over my head, soaped up, and then rinsed off with a couple more pots of water. Bubsy's wife Shanta had put out a special cake of sandalwood soap and I plashed away fragrantly in happy anticipation of my homeward journey.

Not that I was going directly home. I was due to arrive in Bombay at 12:25 that afternoon and take a 1:25 Alitalia flight for Tel Aviv. I would be in Jerusalem that evening for a meeting of the International Society for Metaphysics, where I was to read a paper the next day. On August 23rd I would go to Copenhagen for a day with Kaj and Kitte Baago, Danish friends who had been colleagues at the United Theological College in Bangalore. On the 25th I was booked to Boston. I was due home at 6:45 that evening. In my date book Boston is underlined four times, with two exclamation marks in red after the arrival time. Colombo was the farthest outward point of my journey. From now on, every stop along the way took me closer to home.

I dressed in a shirt, khaki pants, and shoes rather than sandals since I was traveling, packed my suitcase, double-checked to make sure I hadn't left anything, turned off the fan, and opened the door to the living room/dining room. Bubsy and his family were already at the table for breakfast. We had oopoomah, a hot, dry wheat cereal which we ate with our fingers. After breakfast I said goodbye to the children, and Bubsy and Shanta drove me to the airport in his cousin's car. We were early and had a cup of tea before time for my flight. There had been confusion about my reservations a few days before and Bubsy and I had spent several hours in the booking office straightening things out. My ticket was in order now. I had only an hour to change planes in Bombay, however, and as we were saying goodbye the agent announced a thirty-minute delay in the arrival of our flight in Colombo. The announcement made me angry and nervous about my travel plans, but it also made me strangely fearful.

A thin, discordant note of anxiety began an obligato over the chorus of ordinary events.

I bade a fond farewell to the Arulampalams and went through to the waiting area at the gate. I was thinking that I was never going to make the flight to Tel Aviv in Bombay, but I was distracted by a Ceylonese fellow sitting next to me in the departure lounge.

He was a short, squat blob of a man, glistening with sweat, rank with body odor, desperate to talk.

I wanted to worry about my plane connection. Things were out of control and going wrong. I did not want to talk.

He was not offended. He talked for both of us.

It seemed that he now lived in Chicago and worked in mosquito control. I had not previously associated mosquitos with Chicago, nor did I think of the mosquito control crowd as my kind of guys. Mr. Mosquito was undaunted and rattled on.

The departure lounge was crowded and hot, and smelled of perspiration, and ginger flowers, and coconut hair oil, and cigarette smoke. His voice was a reedy counterpoint to the tuneless anxiety I brought to that room. He spluttered about the "goddam bastards" in the bureaucracy in Colombo. Remembering my ticket problems I nodded assent. At least he had that one right. He squeaked on.

"The tax people, my God they are so ignorant, I say I come only for short holiday, and they are telling sorry, sir, you must make deposit for one lakh rupees to guarantee return, and I am telling, my God, one lakh, how I am having one lakh? . . ." Finally our boarding call was announced. I interrupted Mr. Mosquito to say goodbye, and raced for the ramp, somehow thinking that that might get me to Bombay sooner.

On the plane I relaxed a bit. There was nothing I could do now, and the Swiss crew were clearly competent. After a month in India and Sri Lanka, where the incompetence of minor functionaries is the norm, I instinctively believed these attractively crisp and courteous Europeans when they told me that we would take off shortly and easily make up the half hour, arriving on time in Bombay.

We arrived in Bombay forty minutes late. I had to confront my cultural prejudice. The courteous lies of Caucasians are as phony as the loquacious circumlocutions of Orientals.

I had just twenty minutes to make my flight to Tel Aviv. I pushed to the head of the aisle when the door opened and was among the first half dozen or so to get off the plane.

I walked into a blast of heat. I thought at first that it must be from the engines, and then realized that they were shut down. The heat was Bombay in August.

Air India had ground personnel to meet incoming international flights, and at the bottom of the stairway on the tarmac was a man in an Air India uniform with a clipboard, making some sort of announcement as we got off the plane. I pressed my way down the stairs as he repeated his announcement, and as I reached the bottom, I finally heard what he was saying:

"Dr. Rouner; Dr. Lee Rouner: a message for Dr. Rouner."

He even pronounced my name right.

For the briefest instant, I froze on the stairs. The dread of the Colombo waiting room came back. My anxiety had not just been about the plane delay. There was something else. But what? I didn't want to know. At the back of my mind I saw a long mountain ridge with a tiny figure in the middle, outlined against the skyline, faint and far away, fist raised, screaming, "You sonofabitch, go away! Go away, you goddam sonofabitch!"

But what I said was, "I am Dr. Rouner, do you have a message for me?"

He looked up with some surprise.

I don't think he thought there was a real Dr. Rouner.

I think he thought his job was to repeat this sentence until all passengers were off the plane and then report to his office. But he recovered quickly. "This way, please." I thought to myself, "I'm going to miss the plane to Tel Aviv. Why am I following this jerk? Why do we always do this? Some idiot we've never seen before comes up to us and says, 'This way, sir,' and we go. Why? Why do we let these people control us? I don't give a damn about his message, I have to go to Tel Aviv!"

And then immediately I thought, "I hope it's Dad. Let it be Dad. That would be OK. It's time."

The only other emergency message I had had in India was in 1964. My brother had called to say that my father was dying and I'd better come. I flew to New York the next day. He eventually recovered, and he and my mother had a wonderfully happy retirement. But he

28

was in his eighties now, and no one lives forever. That would be OK, I thought.

I didn't want my father to die, because then I wouldn't have him anymore; but I *did* want my father to die because then I wouldn't have him anymore.

I thought again, "Let it be Dad."

The guy from Air India was leading me through the crowd and through turnstiles and waiting rooms which were all a blur, and then to a counter where he gave me a telephone and said that I should call the American Consulate in Bombay, that they had a message for me.

So I called, and said, "This is Dr. Lee Rouner."

The Indian receptionist said, "Who?"

"Dr. Lee Rouner."

"What is your name?"

"Rouner. Dr. Lee Rouner."

"What do you want?"

"I was told that you have a message for me."

"What?"

"I was told that you have a message for me."

"What message?"

"I don't know. Do you have a message for me?"

"What is your name?"

"My name is Dr. Lee Rouner."

Finally she said, "We have no message for a Dr. Rouner."

I hung up, relieved.

I turned to the chap from Air India and told him that they had no message. He seemed undistressed. I learned later that he knew what the message was. He had it there on his clipboard. He was just looking for someone to give it to me.

Then he said, "A Mr. Eric Gass is here. Do you want to see him?" I said, "Of course," with exasperation. Why hadn't he told me that in the first place?

Eric is an old friend. We were missionaries together with the same mission board, and he was now head of the Inter-Mission Business Office in Bombay. We used to see a lot of the Gasses during our summer holidays together in Kodaikanal. Eric looks like Gregory Peck, only more so, and his wife Pat is better looking than he is. I used to tease them about being too beautiful to be missionaries.

Once again the guy from Air India led me through turnstiles and waiting rooms and crowds of curious folk who turned to watch us as we hustled through, wondering what we were about, and then on the other side of a final barrier there were Eric and Pat, strong and still and unsmiling.

I said, "Eric, you have bad news."

Eric said, "Yes."

I said, "What is it?"

He said, "It's Timmy."

I said, "What happened?"

He said, "He's dead."

I said, "No!"

(I thought, *"Don't tell me that!* Tell me it's Dad, I can cope with that. I know about that. That was something that is supposed to happen. Don't tell me it's Timmy.")

"Timmy didn't do anything!"

I slumped against the wall and sank down on a bench, and Pat knelt in front of me and Eric sat next to me with his arm around me, and I just kept saying "No!" "Shit!" and cried, and twisted my body and my hands and my face, trying to get away from it, and escape and be free and have it not have happened, and get back to where I was before, when I didn't know, and there was still Timmy.

Funny Tim, the long, gawky kid who knew how to

take a joke. Timmy who cared about us all, and went to the National Training Laboratory psychology program in Colorado and came home and tried to make a happy family out of two contentious parents. The Tim who came to my study in the evening to talk about his homework, and how the American Indians had the best values, and how we had to get back to that. The kid with the girlfriends, the kid who wrote poetry; the awkward one who seemed embarrassed when you hugged him, but who was always the last one to let go.

"No, for Chrissake NO! Not Timmy, OK? *Not Tim! That's not fair!*"

Pat, kneeling in front of me, holding my hand. Eric, sitting next to me, arm around my shoulders, crying with me. Pat, saying something reassuring. I don't remember what it was, but it was real, and I was glad for her being there, and saying what she said. Gradually I was aware of the Air India guy with the clipboard in the background, and Eric saying, "What do you want to do?"

It seemed like such a strange question. What did I want to do? What did he think I wanted to do? I wanted to go *home*. What else was there to do?

But where was home? Who was home? What had happened? Eric knew only a few details. Timmy had died in Alaska. Rita had gone to Alaska to be with Stephen. Eric did not know when she had gone, whether she was there now, or whether they were all back in Wayland.

Did I want to go on to Zurich? They were holding the SwissAir flight from Colombo for me, because it was going on to Zurich.

Yes, I wanted to go to Zurich.

The Air India fellow gently took my ticket and went to the counter to have it rewritten. He left his clipboard on the bench next to me. It said, "Passenger's son died.

31

American Consul will inform. Passenger will be very emotional."

He returned shortly with my ticket, and assured me that my bag had been put back on the plane. I said goodbye to Eric and Pat, thinking how brave Eric had been in giving me the news straight. I clutched my ticket in one hand and my briefcase in the other and walked from the dark crowded lounge out into the blinding sunshine.

The tarmac was empty, except for a single figure standing far away at the foot of the stairway to the plane. I floated helplessly into the still emptiness, wafted gently by the kindness of Eric and Pat and the Air India man toward the steward at the plane. I did not cry, or think, or feel, or act. I was only conscious of the blazing sun, the endless blue sky, the huge plane, and the tiny figure, waiting patiently.

II

Zurich to Petersburg, Alaska, Wednesday–Thursday, August 17th & 18th

The steward led me up the stairway, through the door and down the aisle to my seat. He stowed my briefcase for me, and after we took off he came and knelt next to my seat on the aisle, just as Pat had done earlier, and asked if he could bring me a little brandy.

I could barely speak, but I shook my head. I didn't want anything to drink; and anyway, I hate brandy. He persisted, confident that it would be good for me, wanting to help. Finally I said I would have some. I didn't want to disappoint him, and his wanting to help really did help.

The brandy was like medicine, and I sipped it slowly. It made me feel sick. I finished it because he had been so kind, and I thanked him. He brought me a paper napkin with the brandy, and I wadded it up in my fist.

For the next few days I always had a wadded paper napkin in my hand, clenching and unclenching, hanging on, spreading it out flat on my knee, folding and unfolding, wadding, clutching, pounding my fist on my thigh, crying quietly. I was swallowed up by this thing that was eating me and I twisted and turned and clutched at it and pounded and tried to get away, and then slumped back for a moment, exhausted, but it loomed over me and ate at me, and I wanted to scream and scream and scream, and run forever, and get away, but I could only go into the lavatory where I was alone, and could cry out, "Oh Timmy!"

I cursed in disbelief. I prayed for Rita and Rains and Jonathan and Christina. I wanted to be with Tim. I thought about the service we would have for him, and how much I needed to do the service myself because it was a way of being close to him.

Timmy was gone.

Something faintly dreaded but totally unexpected now determined everything. All the familiar world images were still there. The clear bright shining was still there, flooding the empty tarmac in Bombay as I floated helplessly toward the plane. But it was no longer like those boyhood lazy summer afternoons at Ossipee Lake, gazing at Mt. Chocorua and Mt. Washington, and the endless blue sunlit sky beyond, when I had been enthralled by its expanse, and freed from the inner constraints of my tight moral world.

Now it was emptiness.

I had never known about emptiness. Even when I was alone, I loved being alone. Loneliness was full of longing, and hope. But now there was a dreadful fact that was never, ever going to be different. I couldn't believe it. I couldn't escape it. Nothing really bad had ever happened to me before, and things could always be made right somehow. If I broke a bone, or wrote a bad term paper, or were mean to someone, I could let the bone heal, or rewrite the paper, or apologize for the meanness.

I am more like my father than I had thought. He really couldn't remember having made an important mistake, but then, I couldn't remember having made a mistake I couldn't fix. "Be ye therefore perfect, as your Father in Heaven is perfect." In our different ways, we both thought we had done that. But now I would never, ever have Tim in my world again. A terrible thing had happened, and I couldn't do anything at all to fix it or make it right. So I wasn't perfect. I was empty and bereft. I was nothing, and Timmy's death was everything.

When we arrived in Zurich I wandered off the plane into the SwissAir lounge. The floors there are glassy black. The transfer counter is at the end of the Swiss-Air wing, and it was hard for me to say what I wanted because I was crying. "My son has been killed in a climbing accident, and I have to get home." The people there tried very hard to get me on a charter flight that was leaving for Boston in a few hours, but the flight was full, and it wasn't possible anyway because of insurance. You can see the runways out the window behind the transfer counter, and I stood by the window in the quiet summer evening and watched that flight taxi out to the runway, past lush green fields in the dying light, and take off.

There is a telephone office just around the corner where there are glass booths. You tell the young woman at the counter where you are calling, and she gets the number for you and then tells you which booth to go to. Afterwards she tells you how much it was and you pay her. When I knew which flight I'd be on the next morning, I called Jonathan in Wayland, and he gave me Rains' number at the police station in Petersburg,

Alaska, and I called. He wasn't there, so I had to call back. I asked him what had happened. I meant, how did Timmy die – was he sick, or did a rock fall on him, or what?

Rains took a long time to tell me all the details of how they made camp and fixed the pitch. The call was costing me about a hundred dollars, so I finally said, "But how did he die?" Then Rains told me about the accident, and how nobody saw him or heard him fall. Rains was very strong, and said how we were all going to be OK. I wasn't OK, and didn't want to be OK, so I didn't want him to say that. But I was glad he was strong, because I wasn't, and I needed him not to be destroyed by this terrible thing.

Then I went to get a ticket to Petersburg at a counter upstairs. It was in a great, empty hall, with a bright light at one end where the ticket counter was. I was helped by an attractive young woman who was very kind and efficient. It seemed like it was very late at night, although it wasn't, really. There was nobody there but the two of us, arranging a ticket to some tiny town I'd never been to on the other side of the world.

I went downstairs afterwards and had dinner at the restaurant right around the corner from the transfer lounge. I ordered a steak because I always like steak, and a beer with it, but I wasn't hungry and I couldn't taste anything, and I didn't finish. About 7:30 P.M. there was a bus to the transit hotel in Zurich, a Holiday Inn. I went up to my room and did situps, and cried and prayed for Timmy, and Rains and Rita and Tina and Jonathan.

Then I went to bed and dreamed over and over about a long vista that was open and filled with sunshine, and at the end there was a high mountain, and Timmy was falling, and I was somehow racing through the air with my arms outstretched to catch him, and then I was holding him and we were falling together but I could feel him next to me, so it was all right.

The next morning I called Jonathan again to tell him that I would stop in Boston, and could he come out to the airport to see me. He said he would, and that some of Timmy's friends had come, and were there in the house in Wayland. Rains' roommate, Scott Ennis, had heard the news while working in Washington on the staff of his senator from Idaho, and left that same day to come to Wayland, and Rains' girlfriend, Tia, was there.

I don't remember getting on the plane in Zurich or what it was like from Zurich to Boston. On that first day I was assailed by my emptiness. I only remember thinking that I would have gone from Colombo to Tokyo if I had known then that I was going to Alaska. I thought, "This sure is the long way home."

The stewardess said I could get off the plane for a few minutes in Boston although we were going on to Chicago, and the other passengers had to remain on board. She took me to the departure lounge, and there were Jonathan and Christina, and Tia and Scott. I gave them all a big hug. Christina said later that she was afraid her daddy was going to cry. She didn't think she could handle that. I didn't cry. She didn't cry either. We all just wanted to be with each other. Nobody knew what to say, or cared about saying the right thing. None of us wanted anything we didn't have right there, because all of us wanted something that we were never, ever going to have again. We were all numbly bound in that, and present to each other.

Jonathan asked if I wanted to talk to Rita. Yes, of course. He'd get her on the phone for me. No, he didn't think he and Christina would come to Alaska with me. They needed time to sort themselves out there at home, and they would be here for us when we got back. He talked to Rita for a moment when he finally reached her at the motel in Petersburg, and then handed me the phone.

"Hi Reet, how are you?"

"I'm OK. How are you?"

"I guess I'm OK. It's hard to tell."

"Yes, I know how that is."

"I'm coming as fast as I can. I'll be there tomorrow at 1:30. Air Alaska from Seattle. I don't remember the flight number but it probably doesn't matter."

"Come soon."

"I will. I love you, Reet."

"I love you too."

"Give my love to Rains and Peter."

"I will."

"Bye dear. See you tomorrow."

"Bye."

Peter was Peter Reilly, Rita's brother-in-law. Peter was in his seventies, British by birth, and had been a climber for fifty-six years. During his last year at Cambridge University, 1923–24, he had been president of the Cambridge University Mountaineering Club. He once told me, "I started two of the Everest climbers, Wyn Harris and Lawrence Wager, on their first rock climb in the Lake District. They followed Mallory and Irving up the northwest face (of Everest), and found an ice axe (but no other sign of what had become of them or whether or not they reached the top before an accident)."

Peter was amazingly fit for his years. He was still an avid downhill skier, white water canoeist and kayaker, and an enthusiast for adventures like the one to Devil's Thumb. When the news of Timmy's death came, Rita's sister Dorry knew instinctively that Rita would want to go to Alaska, and arranged that Peter should go with her. When Rita and Peter eventually got to Anchorage she was on the verge of collapse and it seemed that she might have to be hospitalized. Peter held her for long hours until she recovered her strength. And it was Peter who knew the appropriate questions to ask about expedition planning, so that he could later assure us that they had taken the appropriate precautions, and that Timmy's death was not due to negligence.

Jonathan had a bandage on his right hand. He had been home by himself playing basketball in a summer league, and enjoying a carefree junior-year-of-high-school summer. Rita and Christina had gone with friends to Vinalhaven, Maine, for a few days. Then just before Rita and Christina were due home, the phone rang, and it was Rains, and he told Jonathan that Timmy was dead. Jonathan hung up the phone, went outside in the August morning and smashed his fist through a window in the barn. He was there alone in the house until the next evening when he finally saw the car coming down the driveway, and he went to tell his mother and little sister that Timmy was gone.

Rita got out of the car as Jonathan came slowly down the steps toward her.

"Have you heard from the boys? Are they all right?"

"No."

"What happened?"

"Rains is all right. Timmy's dead."

Tina ran down the driveway, screaming, while Rita shook her head numbly and said, "No, not Timmy!" and Jonathan held her.

I got back on the plane in Boston, shepherded by a flight attendant, blessed in my visit. Almost immediately, however, I was overcome again with loss. In Boston I had concentrated on Jonathan and Christina and Rita, and for a moment I almost forgot why it was that we were all so intense and in need of each other. Then on the plane I remembered. It was like playing football in prep school when I had been "blind-sided" once with a block from behind. One second I was running downfield, and the next I was flat on my back in pain. I didn't know it as I got on the plane, but that was to be the story of the year to come. I would be in the middle of a lecture, or driving home, or talking with a friend, or asleep at night and suddenly the fact that Timmy was gone and was never, ever going to be here again would blind-side me, and once again I would be trying to get away from this awful fact that had become my life, and was keeping me from living.

As I stumbled down the aisle to my seat, I glimpsed a face that seemed oddly familiar. I fastened my seat belt and when we were airborne I caught sight of him again, and wondered if I knew him.

He was a short, squat blob of a man, glistening with sweat. Indian or Ceylonese. Then it came to me. Mr. Mosquito. My companion in the departure lounge in Colombo. He was going home to save Chicago from the mosquitos. I drowsed fitfully for a while, but I had to tell someone what had happened to me. I had no one to talk to. At 37,000 feet over Buffalo, New York, the one person in that hermetically-sealed world whom I knew was Mr. Mosquito; and I had to tell him what had happened. There was a seat open next to his. I went and sat in it. He looked at me blankly for a moment, then brightened and said, "You were in Colombo! Welcome! Welcome! Where you are going? You live in Boston, no?" I started to talk and started to cry at the same time, and he listened while I blurted out that my son had been killed and I was going to Alaska. Finally he said, "I also have trouble. Perhaps we can help each other."

It turned out that he was a Catholic Christian and in Colombo had befriended a young priest, who had accompanied his wife on a trip to Europe the previous spring. He had been suspicious of their relationship, tormented by the thought that they had stayed together in a hotel in Zurich. He had gone to that hotel when our plane landed, and been relieved to discover from the register that they had taken separate rooms. Nevertheless, his relation to his wife continued to be difficult, and he told me all about it.

I've never been very much aware of how I felt, and I've never said much to others about my troubles, so that conversation with Mr. Mosquito was a new experience for me. He told me his story and I told him mine. If he had any wisdom to offer about Timmy I don't remember it, and I know I didn't have any wisdom to offer about his wife. But we each told our stories, and it helped me. He was not my kind of guy, but he was there when I needed him. When we got to Chicago, I thanked him.

I've been to Chicago a number of times since. I don't even know his name so I've never looked him up, but he must be there because the place is still free of mosquitos.

I had several hours in Chicago before the plane to Seattle. I was sitting in the departure lounge two hours ahead of schedule. I didn't know where else to go. I started to shake. It felt like my center was gone. I was literally falling apart. My ground wire was broken. There was all this power surging around willy-nilly, burning out control points in my body. I couldn't move. I couldn't talk. I couldn't do anything. I thought I might collapse there. I sat still and thought about what I had to do.

After a while the shuddering stopped. I got up and walked around, and then it was time to get on the plane.

Seattle was just another airport. I now hate airports. They fill me with dread. They are places of alienation. No one belongs there. They are filled with people "in transit," rushing somewhere else, people who do not care for each other, or even notice one another. They are places where important announcements on expensive address systems are incomprehensible, and ominous. Was that my flight? Are we delayed? Has there been an accident? Is someone trying to reach me? Has someone died?

The death of a child is out of keeping with everything that is supposed to be. Once that has happened, any irregularity is threatening. It becomes a symbol for the One Awful Irregularity that now infects everything. Once, after Timmy died, I lost a contact lens. I was holding it on my finger. Then it wasn't there. I looked again, and it wasn't there. I couldn't believe it. It had been right there. I searched the bureau top, my hand, the floor at my feet; nothing. I was frightened and angry. It had been right there, right in my hand. I didn't shake my hand; I wasn't drunk; I didn't do anything to make it go away. Where the hell was it? For Chrissake, where is my lens? What is happening?

No, no; quick, it will be all right, OK? I will go back to where I started, when I had the lens on my finger, and I will pay attention and make sure that it is still there, and take care of it, and protect it. OK? We can make it right now, can't we? Can't we? . . . No, we can't make it right. No, it is never going to be right, never, ever, ever.

The next morning I took an Air Alaska flight to Petersburg, stopping at Ketchikan and Wrangell. It was a beautiful day. Sitting on the plane, floating over the

44

Rockies, I realized that these mountains were as beautiful as the Himalayas, which I had flown over from Delhi to Kashmir only a few weeks before. The man sitting next to me was about my age, and he had his three boys with him, about the ages of Rains, Tim, and Jonathan. I needed to say something about what had happened to me. It was a survival need, like breathing. It was as though I had to find some way to do it, or I would strangle. I told him that my son had been killed in Alaska, and that I was going there to be with my wife and my eldest son. I told him about getting the news from a missionary friend in Bombay. He asked who the friend was. I said it was Eric Gass. He said, casually, "Oh, I know Eric."

His name was Bob Mensendiek. His brother was a missionary of our Board in Japan, and he knew Eric through his brother. I was amazed and comforted by this small world discovery. He must have been thinking what it would be like to lose one of his own boys, and he empathized with me immediately. But he also gave me some perspective. He said that at least Tim was doing something he loved; so much better than a drunken car crash or dying from drugs, or suicide. I had been so absorbed in my loss that that little bit of common wisdom came as a new insight.

This way of losing Tim was not the worst that could have happened. Several years later I talked with a friend whose son had committed suicide by hanging himself in his room. Desperate for understanding, she had said, "You know what I am going through." But I didn't know anything about that, and was grateful that I didn't. There are some very bad ways to die. Falling off a mountain at nineteen is not one of them. Nineteen is too young to die, but that is not a bad way to go.

The Mensendieks got off at Ketchikan. I nodded goodbye as they gathered their gear and headed out of the airport. They had been more important to me than I was to them, but I didn't care about that. I wasn't even jealous that he still had all three of his boys. I didn't want his boys, I wanted Tim. I was glad that they were going to have a good time, and I had a fleeting picture in my mind's eye of them fishing together out on the river. It was a specific picture of particular people in a definite place, and it helped ground me. For seventy-two hours I had lived in a wild inner world of memory, fantasy, imagination, dream, and speculation all crashing together. The only tangible thing I had to hang on to was a crumpled paper napkin in my hand. For seventy-two hours I had been a little crazy, and I was just beginning to get myself together.

I had forty-five minutes before the plane left for Petersburg. At the north end of the building looking out toward the mountains was a large picture window. I stood there for a long time, staring at the mountains, examining the details of each peak, trying to find out about them.

Were they as wondrous as they seemed, or was that only a trick cloaking some demonic power?

I could not dismiss them as inanimate piles of rock. I knew that that wasn't true. Years before in India, at the end of the Banihal Pass between Jammu and Srinagar, I had come around a curve in the road and suddenly seen the whole Vale of Kashmir spread out below, framed by the snow-covered Himalayas, mirrored in myriad lakes and paddy fields, bordered by blossoming fruit trees, cradled in such moist rolling meadows that England's green and pleasant land seemed conjoined with these heaven-stretching peaks to make a paradise in Asia. Patches of afternoon sun streamed down through broken clouds; death and transfiguration; God's spotlights on his handiwork below.

I could see that the mountains were makers and keepers of the Vale, guardians of a precious treasure. They did not just *seem* majestic to me. Majesty cannot be in the eye of the beholder. It was arrogant foolishness to think that I had the power to endow them with majesty, as some philosophers would have us think. Majesty is the nature of mountain. And I have always trusted that Aristotle was right. Everything that is has its final cause, its purpose in being that kind of thing.

But is there something antagonistic or demonic in the majestic purposiveness of mountains?

Were the mountains to blame for Timmy's death? I had been raised in the mountains of New Hampshire, and loved them.

Could I love them still, or was I bound to hate them for what they had done to Timmy, and to me?

They called my flight, I got back on the plane, there was the inland waterway below, and the mountains beyond, a brief stop in Wrangell, and then we were landing in Petersburg.

I was eager, and afraid: eager to see Rita and Rains, and be comforted by them; afraid they would need me to be strong for them in ways that I could not and did not want to be.

I was like Christina, hoping that her daddy wouldn't cry. I hoped that Rita and Rains wouldn't cry.

The door of the small plane opened, and I walked down the steps to the tarmac. "So this is Petersburg," I thought. "I didn't know they were going to Petersburg."

I had helped Timmy get their train tickets to Prince Rupert, British Columbia, but I didn't know just where they were going after that. I was too busy figuring out where I was going. I hadn't paid attention. Rita was right. I should have known. It wouldn't have saved Timmy, but I should have known.

It brought back all the other times I had not paid attention. It wasn't that I didn't care about him. I wanted to be there for him. I loved his energy, his funky sense of humor, and the way his mind worked. I loved being with him, but there were times when he had needed me and I hadn't noticed. I had been too absorbed in myself, or hadn't realized how important it was to him. And I wondered that I was so scared about climbing.

I can't *believe* I didn't really want to go climbing with him.

I would give anything now if he were only here and we could do our father-and-son thing on some "desperate," and I would love him in the midst of my fear, and claim him in my ineptness, and revel in being his son, and he could be my father, and he would once again call down encouragement to me, and say, "Go for it, Leeroy!" and I would know that he wanted it to go well for me.

Oh, Timmy, c'mon, let's go climbing, OK?

The world was wide and empty, like Bombay, there on the tarmac in Petersburg, and there were Rita and Rains, far away, by the lone airport building.

Rains started loping toward me, just in his shorts and sneakers, running to his father, needing a blessing, needing to be forgiven, needing to know that his world was still intact.

And I needed a blessing.

He wanted to be with me even though I was now defeated and guilty. I could no longer be his hero. I had failed him and Timmy. I hadn't paid attention. Still, he was running to me. His brother had died, and he thought it was his fault. So he ran to me for forgiveness, and I reached out to him for forgiveness, and we clutched

48

each other in that strange, empty place, blessing one another.

"How are you, Rains? I'm glad you're alive."

"I'm OK, Leeroy. I'm glad you're here."

Then we turned and walked with our arms around each other toward Rita, standing awkward and alone, waiting for the Rouner men to include her.

Timmy had been the child with whom she felt closest, the one who looked most like her Rainsford side of the family, one of the few men in her life whom she felt was really for her.

I held her and said, "You've lost your Rainsford child." She nodded numbly, and clung to me.

For a while we all just stood there. I was remembering how special Tim had been for her. He knew it and she knew it. Rita and her father had never been close, even though she had been desperate for a way into his world, and a place in his heart. Because I was much like her father she looked to me as a surrogate doorkeeper to her father's heart-world, but there were many ways in which I prevented that for her. I could be harshly critical of her, and I wanted to write, which did not include her. I was not "really with her," as she put it, in the way that she needed.

In his awkward and unassuming way Timmy had become for her the man she had always longed for. He was her heart's desire, her boon companion on life's way. I acknowledged that in a letter I wrote to Van Halsey, the admissions director of Hampshire College, in the early summer of 1976 after Tim had been admitted there, and they had asked our parent's perspective on their new student.

Mr. Van R. Halsey, Jr.   July 7, 1976
Director of Admissions
Hampshire College
Amherst,
Mass. 01002
      Re: Timothy Nichols Rouner

Dear Mr. Halsey,

Many thanks for your fine letter of June 9, and my apologies for being so late in responding. I'm glad to have a chance to write you about Tim. These will be important years for him, and I have the feeling that Hampshire is just the place for a fellow with his talents, hopes, and hangups.

He is about 6'5", stringy and strong; a rock climber; a very good rock climber as a matter of fact; a rock music fan; a bit of a camera buff, in a modest way; the owner of a 1970 Saab 99, newly purchased for the haggled down sum of two hundred and seventy five big ones, which we figured was not bad even if the transmission is a little shaky, and who the hell knows about the clutch. He is eighteen, but if you catch him profile view in a pensive moment, he looks a lot younger than that. He has energy to spare, hates being bored, and needs always to be moving. Part of him is accommodating, generous, and terribly dear.

He was a beautiful baby . . . and was the most beguiling two-year-old in the history of the human race. And it was evident very early in the game that he was very bright. Sloppy bright; lazy bright; inconsistently bright; but, nevertheless, a fellow with a great deal of intellectual firepower which he has never consistently mastered and mustered.

That's what we want you guys for – and that is what he wants you for, too. Make him get his act together. Make him make decisions and stick to them. Kick his ass in when he is sloppy. Convince him that learning to spell *is* worth his time.

The angel, of course, has another side – rebel in search of a cause. At the White Mountain School he fought the powers that be, largely because they never listened to him, or took him seriously. He wants very much to be engaged with other people, especially – bless his heart – with women. He has a lurking inner fear that he is unable to sustain a real human relationship with friends, especially women.

He is rather prickly, and a bit arrogant, what with all this imaginative energy flowing wide open and full time. I have only just begun to have fights with him, and they are fine times. He does not nurture grudges. He gets mad, and then gets on with the business at hand. He takes the freedom to blow his stack, and gives you the freedom to blow yours.

You need to know something about my wife and me in order to understand Tim. He is more on Rita's wave length than mine. She is an inward spirit, a poet, a dreamer, a worrier. She came from a wealthy family in Westchester County, New York, where religion was something which one did, but with restraint. She bemused the family . . . by deciding to go to theological seminary. She was married by the time she graduated, and immediately became the world's best mother of small children.

(She berates me now for not having paid more attention to them when they were little, but damned if I could think of much to do after she had poured out her enormously creative energy in their direction.) She and Tim share a love of English knights, and "Wind in the Willows," and that *Tintern Abbey* charisma which God gifts to a very few. She is crazy about him in that uninhibited way which mothers have earned the right to, and which cannot but embarrass an eighteen-year-old. But eighteen is a shaky time for even the most stable human being; and the sure knowledge that you are the heart's delight of a woman you know well and admire and love. . . .

I don't know that I ever finished the sentence or the letter, but I wrote it remembering the time I asked Tim whether he ever envied my generation, as having less complicated issues to deal with than his had, and he replied, "Leeroy, the only thing I ever envied of your world was the woman you married." The next day I said to Rita, "I have a present for you," and told her what he'd said.

I remembered that conversation as I looked at her, standing alone at the edge of the tarmac, waiting for the other men in her life to come and be with her.

For me, Timmy was always something of a stranger.

I wrote to Van Halsey that he was more on Rita's wave length than on mine, but that wasn't right. He was more *with* her than with me, but he was really more *like* me than the other children were. We were both second sons, so we could afford to be more lighthearted than our serious elder brother. I think parents tend to gravitate toward the child who is most like the other parent. It's the person you fell in love with, without the flak.

So I always felt an instinctive bond with Rains because he was like Rita – inward, intense, fixed on one idea or one project at a time. I was perhaps overly impressed with that poetic inner world of murky fears and intense longings. It seemed more real than my confident world of moral principles, professional ambition, and indefatigable optimism, which seemed dull by comparison.

Timmy had his own optimism and self-confidence, and there was nothing dull about him. He had had a very happy childhood, and said so several times. He was gregarious, energetic to the point of occasional rowdiness, and hopeful. Ironically, he was something of a stranger to me because he was like me, and I was something of a stranger to myself.

Standing there on the tarmac in the bright sunshine Rains explained that he had wanted Rita and Peter to go to the mountain with him. He wanted to show them where he had been, and the route they had taken, and where Timmy had fallen, and explain what had happened. He needed to explain, explain, explain this inexplicable thing; and we all needed to be part of something we knew we could not participate in.

The weather usually clouds over at that time of year, but it was still clear when Rita and Peter arrived two days earlier, so Rita and Rains had chartered a helicopter and had flown in to Devil's Thumb, fearful that they would miss out if they waited for me. The weather had unexpectedly stayed clear, so they had made arrangements for all four of us to go in that afternoon.

We went into town to the motel where they were staying, and I left my stuff and then we walked the two
miles back out to the airport. On the way Rains told me
how Gary, one of the policemen in town, had let him
stay in the jail for a few days before Rita came, and how
he had shown them the sights around town, and loaned
them his car; and how Charlie Roesel, who was both the
undertaker and the ticket agent at the airport, invited
him to dinner and had befriended him.

As he talked I was taking in the town.

Petersburg is a fishing village on the inland waterway
of the Alaska panhandle. The population seemed to be
a couple of thousand people, and I could see half a dozen
small churches, and guessed that there are probably as
many bars. It is hard to get any place without a small
plane, so there are a lot of amateur bush pilots in town,
and sudden death in high adventure is not unusual. A
friend of Rains' had worked on a fishing boat in Alaska,
so I knew about the sleepless hours, the stench, the
cold, the danger, and the big money to be made in fishing.

This felt like a town dominated by men who lived
with physical hardship and danger; men dependent on
machines; men who slept too little and sometimes drank
too much. At the motel I met Charlie and Pat Roesel's
daughter Shari, a pretty blond teenager, energetically
friendly. I wondered what it was like for her and her
mother in Petersburg. There didn't seem much for a
woman to do except "stand by her man."

But I was struck with the gentleness of the men Rains
had met. It reminded me of home in Sandwich, New
Hampshire, where men work in the woods, and plow
snow in the winter, dependent on chain saws and bull-
dozers, which too often cut them or kill them. They, too,
are extraordinarily gentle, kind, and uncompetitive,

unlike the more educated professional men in the city who are gracious, polite, and aggressive.

The airport had a single runway, and off to one side was a helicopter pad, and a low building with a sign which read TEMSCO HELICOPTERS, INC. The proprietor was a medium-sized, squarely built fellow in his fifties named Earl, wearing a TEMSCO cap, plaid shirt, and suspenders on his gray work pants. He greeted Rita, Rains, and Peter with gruff familiarity and gave my hand a friendly shake. They had two choppers. We were waiting for the larger one which could take all four of us. The pilot's name was Bob, and he was out on another job, but due back soon.

We hung around for a bit making small talk and then heard a droning "whap-whap-whap" in the distance. A few moments later the sound was all around us, and the chopper popped over the tree tops, and slipped down toward the pad, tilted slightly backwards, like a runner sliding into base, fanning up dust and debris and finally righting itself just as it settled.

Bob turned off the engine, climbed down, and had a word with Earl. He was well muscled and fit, wore work boots, blue jeans, and a tan flannel shirt. He had reddish hair, a square, open face and was in his late twenties. He walked over to the building with Earl, and a few minutes later came back and told us to climb in.

Rains and Rita and Peter crammed themselves in the back, since they had seen the view on their earlier trip. I sat up front next to Bob. He had gone to the University of Minnesota, and had come to Alaska looking for a job after college. He didn't know what to say about Timmy's death, but he was friendly and helpful and I liked him.

55

I had never been in a helicopter before. The noise was so loud we had to shout to be heard, even though we were only inches away from each other. Take-off was abrupt, with the chopper tilted sideways like a young heron just learning to fly. Immediately below us were dark green pines and the dark blue, wind-rippled waterway, but as we flew inland from the coast toward British Columbia there were snow-covered mountains all around us. Eventually, we came to the edge of the Baird Glacier, and followed it to its beginnings in the Witch's Cauldron at the base of Devil's Thumb.

On the way we crossed a river at the edge of the glacier where the chopper had met Rains and Peter Cole after their climb. The pilot had been sent to pick up three climbers and their gear. When only two appeared he asked about the third. That was the first of many times when Rains had to explain what had happened, tell his story and watch people's reactions to it, and see if he had been able to make it comprehensible to them, so that he could belong in their world of understanding; or whether it was beyond them, or rejected by them, so that he would have to live outside their world.

I was beginning to feel how impossible Timmy's death must be for him; impossible to explain; impossible to live with; impossible to share.

Devil's Thumb dominates the landscape for miles around, appreciably higher than the surrounding peaks. On Air Alaska flights from Anchorage to Seattle, pilots often point it out as a landmark. Bob put the chopper down close to where their campsite had been on the glacier at the base of the mountain. We all clambered out, and stood there taking in the scene.

The weather was warm. I had been wearing a blue Levi work shirt and carried a red ski sweater, but I never needed it. There was no wind, and the tempera-

ture was around sixty-five. The glacier was rutted with
deep cracks every twenty or thirty feet. The snow on
the surface was soft in the August sunshine, but there
was firm crust only an inch or so down, and hard ice under that. Because we were right underneath it, the view
of Devil's Thumb was foreshortened, but the mountains
on the rim of the Witch's Cauldron were in perspective.

The Witch's Cauldron is a semi-circle of peaks at the
beginning of the Baird Glacier with Devil's Thumb in
the center, so named because rock, ice, wind, and snow
are constantly astir on the rim of that enormous geo-
logical bowl.

The sky was crystal blue and cloudless, with the sun
almost overhead. The glacier was spotted with large
chunks of broken rock from the mountain. As I was
wondering how the broken rock got there, the first of
a regular series of large booming noises came from high
in the surrounding peaks. I looked up to the right and
saw a great plume of snow swirling upward, and a
cascade of ice, snow, and rock flowing down the side of
a far peak toward the floor of the glacier. Before long
there was another boom, and a great crystalline geyser
shot into the air at the source of a new stream of ice and
rock threading its way down the irregular slope. Behind it all was the benign passivity of the endless blue
sky, and the perfect brilliance of sunshine making snow
plumes translucent, cascading rock and ice bejeweled,
and the summit of Devil's Thumb radiantly Olympian.

Death and transfiguration, again; agony and ecstasy.

I said to Rita, "I can see why these guys wanted to
come."

She nodded assent, but I knew it was different for
her. She loved the mountains and had first introduced
the boys to climbing when they were little. Her inward-
ness has its own ecstasy, but it is not the ambitious

ecstasy of magnificent achievement. It is the lyrical ecstasy of received blessing from nature, or a friend. These death-defying mountaineering expeditions were strange and fearsome to her.

The broken ice axe in the trunk of the Benz was a symbol of that.

Why did they have to do this?

What did they need to prove?

She and I had often seen Peter Cole's slides. He is a professional photographer, and gives shows in places like the Appalachian Mountain Club or the Harvard Outing Club, with low-key narration and taped musical accompaniment. His shows regularly included a good many pictures of Rains in Yosemite, or British Columbia. The mountains were glorious beyond any singing of it, and there would be Rains in a sleeping bag, pinned to the wall of a sheer cliff with only a couple of pitons holding him, three thousand feet above the ground, reading T. S. Eliot, with Beethoven in the background.

Awesome.

I was jealous of something I would love to do but didn't have the guts for, and was too old for anyway. Rita seemed equally impressed with the insouciance of climbers facing danger, but it wasn't something she wanted to do, and she always wondered why they wanted to do it.

For me, going to the mountain was a reward, the unlocking of a secret. Timmy and Rains and Peter Cole had often sat around our kitchen table over beers and said how being in the high mountains was awesome, and I believed it, but I hadn't been there, so I had to take their word for it. Now I was there, and I knew why they wanted to come.

Rains and Rita and Peter Reilly and I stood together in the shadow of the mountain. Rains pointed out their route to us, and gradually the pieces of the story began to fit together. They had taken the train from Montreal to Prince Rupert, then gone by small float plane to Ketchikan, and by a regular Air Alaska flight from Ketchikan to Petersburg. In Petersburg they hired a TEMSCO helicopter to take them in to the campsite, and arranged for the helicopter to pick them up two weeks later at the river on the edge of the Baird Glacier. They had no radio for communication with Petersburg, but a radio wouldn't have done them any good, since they were surrounded by peaks.

They had spent the first two days in camp getting organized and examining the mountain with field glasses for the best route, since no one had climbed the northwest face before. On the second day Rains and Timmy had fixed the first pitch, which means that they had placed ropes on the first cliff so that they could all get a fast start on the difficult first part by simply climbing up the ropes, a technique called "jewmaring." On the third day they started up.

They got up the rope section quickly and then discovered that the next part was easier than it had looked from below. By mid-afternoon they were almost a third of the way up the peak, and the climbing had been unexpectedly easy. Much of it was more like a steep hike than technical rock climbing and late that afternoon Peter remarked casually, "We haven't had to think all day."

About five o'clock in the afternoon, with the sun still fairly high—it was August 3rd—they crossed a flat snow field. At that point the snow field became quite steep. Now they did have to think.

They had not been roped up. Rains said to Peter, "Shouldn't we rope up?" Peter suggested that they wait until they got to the top of the next pitch.

Peter went first, Rains followed him, and Tim came last, the safest position. Peter was soon out of sight. Rains focused on following in Peter's steps, jamming his crampons in for firm footing, and using his ice axe for security as he made his way up the steep slope. It was hard work, and he was scared. He thought that maybe they should have roped up, but he didn't want to seem chicken, or hold them up. He was sweating lightly under his down jacket for the first time that day.

They had agreed to climb separately as far as a large rock outcropping about four hundred yards up the slope. By the time Rains reached the rock Peter had already gone on ahead, but Rains settled in to wait for Tim. He took off his pack, caught his breath and took in the spectacular view, flushed with the achievement of this high point on the mountain.

After a while he thought, "Where the hell is Tim?"

He got up, moved around the rock, and looked back down the slope. He could see only a few yards of their trail before the slope dropped off.

Nothing.

"Shit."

Annoyance; surprise; anxiety.

"C'mon Nichols. Let's go. It's getting late. . . ."

He put his pack on, climbed back to where the slope dropped off, and looked further down the trail.

Nothing.

"What the hell . . . ?"

Rains moved quickly now, back-climbing down the slope. What happened to Tim? Broke a crampon, probably. Sitting there saying words Reet wouldn't approve. Took a breather half way up? Not likely. He fell? Oh, *shit!* No, he would have slid straight back down the slope. He's OK. . . .

Where the hell is he, for Chrissake?

60

Then he turned and saw it.

Just a feature of the trail, beside the regular series of boot prints.

Nothing dramatic in itself.

Nothing to mar radically the lovely sweep of slope, the awesome reach of skyline in the Witch's Cauldron, the glories of late afternoon August sunlight slanting down on what Tim had once called "these great high peaks of the Spirit."

It was a small thing, really.

A sitzmark in the snow, just to the right of the trail on the cliff side, and then a three-foot swathe in the snow, like a skimobile track, only not so smooth, which led to the edge of the cliff, and over.

In an instant so immediate as to make the telling of it seem forever, Rains' heart slid down the swathe to the edge of the cliff, intact but swelling as it slid, and when it reached the edge, his heart burst, and all its tiny drops of blood exploded outward to the horizon, and upward to the fast-dying radiance of the setting sun, and down to the abyss below.

He slumped into the side of the slope, jammed his ice axe into the snow, rested his forehead on the gentle curve of the axe, and cried.

Just for a moment.

Then he was full of cold, reckless energy.

With his left hand he jammed the sharp point of the axe handle into the snow, while he grabbed for his hammer with his right and pounded the ice axe furiously into the ice beneath. He uncoiled the rope from over his shoulder, tied it to the axe, and started to rappel over the edge of the cliff. Looking down he saw Tim's body, motionless, on a ledge some two hundred feet below.

He knew he was dead.

In the cold fury of his descent, that was only a con-

firming item of information, a meager empirical foot-
note in the vast volume of his exploded heart.

The rope ended about twenty feet above the ledge.

He let go, crashed to the ledge, scrambled to the still
warm but lifeless body of his brother, held him, kissed
his face, moaned, "Oh, Tim! Goddamit! Shit! Oh Nichols!" rocked back and forth, his face pressed against his
brother's.

He lay next to Tim for a long time. When he finally
looked up, the sun had gone down.

III

Petersburg
August 19th–20th

Rains put Tim's body in his sleeping bag up against the cliff wall so that it would be out of the way of falling rock and ice. Peter came soon after that, and they stayed that night on the ledge. When they went down the next morning Rains took Tim's helmet and boots and camera with him.

They had ten days before the helicopter would be back to pick them up. Ten days with nothing to do but wait. Ten empty days, pierced with the incredible nothingness of Timmy's not being anymore.

Rains wrote in his journal, and stared up at the mountain where Timmy lay cold and unmoving on the ledge. He talked to Peter some, but mostly he wandered around the glacier near their campsite, picking up big chunks of the broken rock which lay everywhere, piling them together to make a huge cairn. The rock was white diurite, much like the New Hampshire granite he knew so

well. It was something to hang on to, something to do;
the strain of lifting the boulders, then stumbling under
their weight to the pile, letting go, hearing their dull
crack as another lifeless body crashed on this recon-
structed mountain and finally rested there, cold and
unmoving.

When our chopper landed, and I saw the cairn, I wondered how it had been for Rains to pile all those rocks
there.

Did he fling them angrily, or lower them gently, or
just drop them?

The cairn was a labor of love, but love harbored despair
and guilt, loneliness and loss, all jumbled together. The
cairn seemed less a testimony of devotion to Tim than
to the enormity of his death and the laborious struggle
with it which had become Rains' life. Sweating and grunt-
ing under those back-breaking boulders seemed less a
gesture of farewell than a fight against farewell.

Cradle him home.

Kill yourself so he won't be killed.

Make a new mountain,

More real than Devil's Thumb.

Don't let the bastards win this one.

"Bring him back, for Chrissake!

"I want him back!"

The last rock he brought to the cairn was probably not
flung furiously, or lowered gently. I imagine that the last
rock was just dropped there, dispiritedly, clunking on
one or two others before rolling back onto his foot, exact-
ing a minor pain, a small bloody scrape on his shin, and
a sense of defeat.

I can see him extracting his foot with disgust, mutter-
ing "Shit," turning away, and then sitting on a rock to cry,
some place where Peter couldn't see him, and where he
wouldn't have to be comforted, or explain what he was do-

ing with the rocks, and why he cared, and what it meant, and why he really couldn't explain anything at all.

Rita had brought flowers for us to put on the cairn as a memorial to Tim. We stood there quietly for a moment, Rita and Rains and Peter Reilly and I, and then I said a prayer for Tim, and for us all. Peter and I wandered off toward the chopper after that, and talked with Bob about the dangers of flying in these mountains, but Rita and Rains stayed at the cairn, crouched together, clinging to one another.

Each had lost the one person in their world whom they needed most.

Then we gathered near their campsite and Rains pointed out the details of the route they had taken on the mountain, and told us how they decided not to rope up when they came to the steep place where Timmy eventually fell.

In telling his story Rains offered no excuses, made no apologies, and blamed no one. Like a surgeon operating on his own child, removed from his anguish, he cut cleanly and simply to what had happened. Like Eric giving me the news straight in Bombay. I loved Rains for that. I didn't want to hear how he felt about it, not then. I just needed to know what had happened.

Peter Cole was not as gifted a rock climber as Rains, but he was older, more knowledgeable, and had had much more experience on big mountain mixed rock and ice climbs of this sort. This was Tim's first expedition on a major peak. I don't know anything about that kind of climbing, so I was grateful to Peter Reilly, who knew all the right questions to ask Rains about their preparations, equipment, nature of the climb, and so forth.

I don't know why Timmy fell, and I never will. No one saw it happen, or heard anything. When Rains found his body he had a fractured skull, a broken neck, and a broken leg. The medical report later said that he died instantly. Did he break his leg first, somehow? Or did the soft snow ball up under his crampons so he couldn't get proper footing? That's the best guess, but no one really knows.

Was it a mistake not to rope up?

Probably, but you can't be sure.

What's the choice? Between Timmy living or dead?

Well then, Yes, it *was* the wrong call.

Between having all three dead and Timmy dead?

Well then, No, it wasn't.

(Three climbers were killed in Alaska in another accident a few weeks later, and they were roped together.)

My mother used to say, after disasters large and small, "If we had only known . . ." It made me angry to hear her say that because we couldn't know and we knew we couldn't know, and I have ever since hated that kind of omnipotent second-guessing, and the spiritual self-flagellation that goes with it.

But I needed the truth in order to survive, and I knew I could never be close to Rains again unless we were true with each other. I remembered an old Gospel hymn from childhood, "I would be true for there are those who trust me." It had been the theme song of my strenuous youthful moralism, the anthem of my arrangement with God whereby I would be good and He would protect me. But even as that covenant was crumbling, I discovered that the truth could save me. It was my only protection against a life of fear and furtiveness.

I knew I was strong. I knew I could cope with the pure, awful loss of Timmy. New England Puritanism is geared for that. But it would have to be clean. I couldn't cope if it was going to be dank and festering, smeared with guilt, hushed up and hidden away. There was no house big enough for me to live in if this enormous presence were to squat ominously, unrecognized, threatening, in our midst, like a huge fetid toad in the living room which everyone walked around and no one mentioned because we had all agreed to pretend that it wasn't there.

I knew I wasn't strong enough to do that.

Sooner or later I would be depressed, then physically ill. Only the truth could save me from sickness and death. I needed to know what was true about my relation to Timmy, and his death; I needed to know truly how I felt in the midst of it all; and I needed to tell Rains what I really thought about his sense of guilt.

If Rains had questioned the decision in his mind but never said anything to Peter Cole, he could then have said to himself, "I should have said something," and he would be right. But he did say something. He trusted Peter's judgment, with good reason, and accepted it. He used to call Peter Cole "Pops." Father and son. Dominant and subordinate. After the fact, knowing what he knew, Rains felt he should have insisted. Stand up to the dominant male authority.

OK, Rains, maybe so. But you might all be dead.

After a disaster we think it could have been avoided by changing the one thing that we now see as the cause. We forget that changing one element changes everything, and there is no way to predict that new situation, any more than it was possible to predict the old one. Hindsight is never as revealing as it is cracked up to be.

Sorry, Mother. Even if we had known, it might not have done us any good.

None of us knows the future, Rains. Beware the seductions of my mother's yearning for omniscience, and your own passion for self-blame.

You did the best you knew at the time.

Why do you need to be better than that?

OK, I can guess.

But let me tell you, Rains, my father and me to the contrary notwithstanding, most mortals make mistakes. If that was a mistake.

And you and I still have enough of Dad in us so we think that hard work and good motives will make things turn out right for us, and when they do we think we made it happen. You and I have had a lot of good fortune, and we forget how much of it is really just good luck. So when we have bad luck, we think we made that happen, too.

To admit accidents is to acknowledge that I cannot control everything. Guilt says things would have been OK if only I had done what I could have, and should have, but somehow didn't.

I choose guilt.

I'd rather feel guilty than helpless.

But nothing bad had ever happened to me before, so why should I believe in bad things any more than my father?

I was the moral ruler of my own universe.

Le Roi.

I also ruled out incomprehensibility. I am a philosophical Idealist, convinced that there is a reason for everything, and that if I work hard enough on the details of my own experience I can figure out what is going on and why.

That seemed in keeping with the idea of God's Plan. I always thought I could understand my little corner of the Plan if I worked hard enough at it. But incomprehensibility is the nature of accident, Rains, and I now suspect that God is the only one who understands God's Plan. When people asked Karl Barth theological conundrums, he used to say, "God only knows." I like that better than I used to.

70

So, are you guilty, Rains?

I don't know.

I only know that, for myself, I lust after guilt.

Every movie I see about the Russian purges or the Chinese Cultural Revolution gives me a warm rush whenever former leaders confess sincerely to things they didn't do. The logic is flawless. Since they were responsible for all the good things before, they must be responsible for all the bad things now, right? I'm with those guys. That's my version of wanting to have it all and thinking I can control it all. Maybe I was a Chinese Emperor in the last life. Concupiscence, as Tillich called it, is my thing.

Lust.

And guilt is my favorite way of maintaining it.

It may be different with you, Rains. If you had a real moral choice which you screwed up, you really are guilty, and need to say so and be forgiven. But I didn't hear that in your story.

Accidents happen.

Timmy chose the risks, and made a mistake.

(What do you suppose actually happened when he fell . . . ?)

I think he had an accident, that's all.

We didn't have a lot of time at Devil's Thumb, helicopter rentals being what they are, and Bob brought out the chopper's cargo net which Rita had asked him to bring. On their first trip in Rita wanted to bring out a piece of the mountain to use as a headstone for Timmy's grave, but they didn't have the net. She often had good ideas like that and immediately proposed them. They were often things that I would not have thought of, or might have thought vaguely at the back of my mind but would not have pushed for. I am too passive

71

in situations like that. Immediately I loved the idea,
and we all embarked on a search for exactly the right
rock. There were numerous candidates before someone
found The One which Rita approved, and we loaded it
into the cargo net, slung beneath the helicopter. Then
it was time for us to take a last look at the mountain
before heading home.

We scrambled into the chopper, and lumbered into
the air, gaining altitude by circling laboriously, since
the chopper was overloaded. All the while I was looking
at our shadow on the ground far below. There was the
chopper, like a dragonfly with spinning wings overhead,
and below us in the cargo net a long motionless object
which looked for all the world like Timmy's body. I knew
that the Mountain Rescue Squad had flown in several
days before to bring Tim's body out in a cargo net, but
I felt then as though we were doing it again. It was our
version of Rains building the cairn. Re-enact the drama.
Make it come out right this time.

We were bearing Timmy out on his shield. The dead
warrior, flying over the Alaskan Rockies, not in triumph
or disaster, but with the glory befitting one who has
died in the mountains. We knew he was dead, and that
he could never be for us again, but at least for the moment he was with us, and he was ours, and we were his,
forever.

The mountain was dark wet with the late August
run-off from the snow. Bob tried to get us as close as
possible, and I tried to take pictures so that we would
have some record of the occasion and what the mountain looked like. The noise of the chopper was intense,
and Rains was yelling and pointing that that was the
place. I was anxious and confused, fumbling with the
camera and trying to be sure I was taking pictures of
the right place. After a couple of passes at the moun-

tain I wasn't able to feel very much anymore, so I was glad when we stopped circling and zooming in on a place which suddenly seemed unimportant and headed back to Petersburg.

We took a different route back, and flew directly over the mountains rather than down the glacier. It was beautiful to see the peaks, and the unblemished snow, and the endless blue sky beyond, and whenever I looked down there was the shadow of the chopper and the rock beneath us in the cargo net, and I couldn't shake the thought that we were taking Timmy home.

Bob landed the chopper very gently, knowing that the rock might break, and knowing how much it meant to us. Beginning as a grim reminder, the rock soon took on many of Timmy's characteristics. It became a comic character, a handsome *persona,* a sprightly presence.

We had decided that the only way to get the rock home safely was to ship it by air freight and have it properly crated beforehand. Send it by Railway Express and it takes forever, gets handled every couple of days, and is sure to break sooner or later.

The rock was, in fact, fairly flat and thin. If you propped it on one end, it looked eerily like Devil's Thumb, and we figured that that was exactly what we would do with it. There is a graveyard at the foot of our driveway at High Meadow Farm in North Sandwich, New Hampshire. The rock would be the headstone for Timmy's grave. And it would face west, toward the Rockies, the "great high peaks of the Spirit."

Petersburg is a small town and people had seen us on the street, going to dinner, or heading out to the airport, and they were very good to us. Some of them stopped us to say that they had heard about our trouble, and were real sorry, and if there was anything they could do for us, all we had to do was just say so. We thanked them and told them that they had just done a whole lot for us by stopping to say what they did, and we were grateful, and glad to be among such kind people.

But I imagined that they couldn't quite figure the rock.

"I mean, they must have rocks back there in New England, dontcha' think?"

"My God it's gonna cost 'em to ship that baby all the way to Massachusetts. Lookit it, all crated up (you know, them crates cost, too) and that balsam twig stuck in it like it was a present for somebody!"

"Geez, they must have money, hiring helicopters every day and sending off rocks by air freight to Massachusetts!"

The young fellows who crated the rock for us had to bring it to our motel in the back of their pick-up to make sure they had done it the way we wanted. When we said that it looked great to us, they were pleased and drove back through town on their way to the airport, with this well-crated rock prominently displayed on the tailgate, bearing its sprightly sprig of balsam for all the bemused citizenry to see.

I could just see Timmy's grin, and feel him itching to do his imitation of local folk making wisecracks about the rock. He had perfected a "down Maine" accent by memorizing a number of Marshall Dodge's *Bert and I* stories, and he would entertain family and friends with his uproarious imitations.

His style was rowdy and exaggerated. Jonathan is the quickest wit in the family, and would make a great stand-up comic in the early Bob Newhart tradition. Timmy, on the other hand, was something out of the old days of vaudeville, a lusty fellow with slapstick in his soul, a "Keep on Truckin'" type. There was a touch of the Marx Brothers in Tim. And he was into local color because he was into locals.

Timmy hated pretension and superficiality, and he loved ordinary folk because they were honest and could say what they thought. He was critical of the academic culture he had experienced, because he thought it tended to make people dishonest and manipulative with both their ideas and their feelings. He wrote a senior thesis at the White Mountain School, evaluating several experimental private secondary schools. The title was "Too Much Success; Not Enough Happiness." Rita was his advisor on that project, and they fed each other's anti-establishment convictions.

Tim was afraid that conventional education made people less direct with themselves and others, less able to know their own minds, and pursue their own goals. He thought it reduced language to jargon, and left people unable to express clear, strong, original ideas. During his freshman year at Whitworth College in Spokane, Washington, he was critical of the students for being "phony." They couldn't say what they thought or how they felt. With his eastern, teenage, smart-ass arrogance, he once said that they "talked like they were on some California TV show."

The locals, on the other hand, knew how to talk.

I did the funeral of Jesse Ambrose, a neighbor in North Sandwich, and Timmy loved my favorite Jesse story. Jesse died in his nineties, in the same room where he had been born, in a farmhouse in Whiteface Intervale. He went to the New Hampton School in the era when Shakespeare and the Bible were still literary staples, but he never went to college, and he spent his life on the land as a farmer. He was a Republican, like everyone else around here, and in 1963, with a particularly crowded field in the New Hampshire primary, Jesse was interviewed by *TIME* magazine, seeking his views on the campaign.

Jesse confessed, in his New Hampshire twang, that "the issues are such as to befuddle the bucolic mind."

Jesse knew how to talk.

Timmy loved the story for Jesse's eloquence, but especially for his articulate honesty. Jesse knew how to say "I'm confused" with natural grace, a self-deprecating sense of humor, and a needle for the New York City reporter, all in the same brief sentence.

Adolescent kids struggle with mixed emotions, and Tim, at eighteen, needed folk who had their emotions straightened out, and could say how they felt. One of his closest friends in the year or so before he died was Bud Staples, who was our caretaker in North Sandwich, because Bud was an honest man. So Timmy mastered the local accent and metaphor, and pranced through his great stories about Bud, and Jesse, and I could just see him up there among the gods entertaining one celestial assembly after another with tales from *Bert and I,* and wishing the hell he could come down and do us his own Newly Perfected Petersburg Perusal of the Transcendentally Reincarnated Rock.

"And Now, Ladies and Gentlemen;

"Straight from Valhalla,

"Risen from his Shield,

"The Missing Marx Brother,

"The Notorious Nichols Himself!"

And he would come on and start in:

"Lemme tell ya' about these folks from Boston. They had kids who was just dying to come out here and get theirselves killed in the mountains, dontcha' know, so they did, and they figured what they needed as a memento of this auspicious occasion was a rock . . ."

O Timmy, where are you when we need you? You son-ofabitch, come on back and be with us, OK?

When we got back to Petersburg from Devil's Thumb we made arrangements to have the rock crated, and then said goodbye to Bob and Earl. As we came out of the office Rains nodded toward a fellow who was painting the flagpole by the landing pad. He was the pilot who had flown in the rescue team that brought out Tim's body. Rains had wanted to give him something, and the word was that a bottle of bourbon would be much appreciated.

His name was Jack. He had dark hair, a ready grin, and a firm handshake. Rains introduced me to him, and I said, "I want to thank you for what you did for us." He laughed a bit ruefully, and said, "I was scared to death the whole time." When I heard the story, I could see why.

As soon as Rains had been able to get to a phone he had reported to the Alaska State Police that his brother's body was still on the mountain. The police organized a volunteer rescue team of climbers in the area to bring Tim's body out. Rains was desperate to go with them—his last chance to help his brother; a chance to be near him; a chance to do something, after just waiting for so long.

When the team flew in the next day from Anchorage he took his climbing gear to the airport. He told them that he was an experienced climber, he knew the terrain, which they didn't, and hell, it was his brother. He had a right to go. But the State Police said No. They were afraid he would be too emotional. Rains knew how coldly calculating he had been at the moment of Tim's death, but he couldn't convince them.

So he stood alone by the pad, while the three climbers loaded their gear, and then he watched the chopper slide up into the cloudless sky and bee-line out over the inland waterway, like a heavy-headed arrow, aimed straight at the heart of Devil's Thumb.

The rescue was complicated because Tim's body lay on a narrow ledge, and there was no place to land within easy climbing distance. The strategy was to bring the chopper close to the side of the cliff so that one pontoon could rest on the ledge while the climbers got out, recovered the body, and secured it in the cargo net. Holding the chopper steady with only one pontoon touching down was problem enough. But the cliff wall was only a few feet from the chopper blades. A downdraft would blow the chopper off the mountain. An updraft would blow it into the mountain. Either possibility put lives at risk; all just to bring out a dead body.

I'm amazed that total strangers would do that.

Maybe climbers, like soldiers in battle, feel honor-bound to bring out their dead. But they didn't know Timmy or Rains. And I never did know who they were. They had been climbing in other parts of Alaska and the call went out over the State Police radio.

Any volunteers to rescue a climber's body?

Hey, OK.

So they did the job with the casual macho of skilled risk takers, and then went back to their climbing. Perhaps, like soldiers in battle, it is just one more risk in a risky life. Maybe even welcomed. Part of the climber's code. Hey, no sweat, man.

But now, eleven years later, I am ashamed that I never tried to find out who they were, and thank them. And I don't think the climber's code explains what they did.

Yes, they were reclaiming one of the fraternity of

those who dance with death, so they were doing it for one of their own; but they were not unlike those ordinary people who risk their lives instinctively for strangers in car accidents and drownings and everyday crises of all sorts. What awes me is this instinctive caring of people for each other.

Jack had to ferry the climbers up from the glacier floor to the ledge, and then take Tim's body down to the glacier floor before going back for the climbers, so he made that risky landing not once, but three times, in shifting winds. They found Tim's body in the sleeping bag where Rains had left it, right up against the side of the cliff, out of the way of falling rock and ice. They tied it into the cargo net, and clipped the net into the net rings under the chopper. Jack ferried the body down to the glacier, and then went back up for the rescue team.

They climbed in while Jack held the chopper steady on one pontoon. Then he veered off from the mountain and soared into the safety of the open sky. They picked up the cargo from the glacier, and headed up over the ridge and back to Petersburg, with the long shadow of Tim's body fleeting across snow fields and rocky peaks beneath them.

I think of Jack, gratefully, whenever there is talk about the Right Stuff, and I sent him another fifth of bourbon from Rita and me to say so.

We walked the two miles back into Petersburg. I was glad to have my feet on the ground, after the tilting and swooping of the chopper. I needed some quiet to absorb the drama of the day after the roaring of engines, the crashing of mountain avalanches, and the thunder in my own blood. The weather was just what I needed.

Clouds came in toward evening, and it was cool and dank as we trudged along through marshland. The salt-sea smell was heavy in the air, and nothing was stirring.

In Bombay I had told Eric that I wanted to go home, and I wasn't sure who was home or where home was, everyone being scattered. I felt instinctively that I wanted to be with Rita, and that home was with her. And now we were together, but this terrible bond was also a separation. Our Tim had died, but her Tim was not my Tim. I hadn't smoked pot with him when she and Tim had camped together in Maine; and she hadn't skied with us when Tim and I had gone to Waterville together. My talks with him had not been her talks. We were different people and we had a different relation to a Tim who was different for each of us. So I couldn't be at home with both him and her without recognizing that we were all different, and that our relations were all different.

But I couldn't bear difference, at least not right then. I wanted home to be a melding together. I wanted to be identified with her and with him, but I knew immediately that that was not possible, and that there was distance between us.

We went back to the motel and sat around before dinner in our cramped room, drinking beer and talking about what had happened to each of us during the time we had been separated: me in India, Rains in Alaska, Rita in Wayland, and Peter in North Sandwich. We didn't talk about how we felt. We just said what had happened. I wanted to know details, so that I could have something to hang on to. I was drowning in a sea of feeling, and simple facts were life preservers, keeping me afloat. I could not cope with how I felt, but if I could just hang on to the details maybe I could ride out the feeling till I knew what to do.

I drank a lot of beer.

I wasn't trying to forget, or get out of anything. I was trying to get into it. I was like the high divers at Quincy Quarry in the summertime, soaring out and down toward the one deep spot between the shallow ledges just below the surface of the water. I wanted to plunge into that dark hole, and explore the murky secret of what this was all about.

"Did somebody *mean* to do this?

"Did I do something wrong?

"An accident? What *is* an accident? I don't really understand."

Having lost what felt like everything, I could risk everything. So I roared about in my inner, empty dark, shouting, "Hey, I mean, screw it, man, what is really happening?" And all I got back was, "I don't know, man, I don't know."

We went out to dinner at a place in town noted for seafood, and we all ate an enormous amount and still felt empty. Afterwards we walked along the beach back to the motel in the waning evening light, with the ocean lapping quietly at the shore and the fishing boats in the harbor undulating gently as the Bay of Alaska heaved and sighed and gathered her scattered children into her oncoming dark.

All four of us were in the same room. Rains and Peter had the two beds. Rita and I slept on the floor. When we were finally in bed I reached out to her instinctively.

I wanted to be melded, not separated.

I wanted it to be us together, against this awful thing that had happened to us.

So we came together, and loved each other with our bodies, furtively in the dark, with Rains and Peter lurking above us in their beds, breathing heavily in exhausted sleep. And I plunged down into that deep

81

place, seeking an answer in the warm dark. But there was no answer. It was a momentary touching of lovers from different worlds, who knew how much they belonged together, how different they were, and how much they needed from each other something they would never get.

The next morning we went out to breakfast at a place where Rita and Rains had been before, which featured a "Lumberjack Special"—large orange juice, oatmeal with heavy cream, a six-layer stack of pancakes, with butter, maple syrup, a generous helping of bacon or ham, and a bottomless cup of coffee. I had it all, even after the huge dinner the night before. We all ate like that for the five days we were in Petersburg, and no one gained a pound. Our bodies seemed to be living two separate lives, like our minds.

Outwardly I was going about my business, taking care of details, even occasionally having fun as we did that afternoon when we went for a long walk and a swim. But inwardly a wild beast was loose, threatening to devour me, eating at my vitals (not to mention my Lumberjack Special). For months I was always physically tired and mentally forgetful from this double life of living day to day, and fighting the beast within. And I was always a little hungry.

That day Rita and Rains and I went for a long walk along the outskirts of the town. Everywhere there were views, and always Devil's Thumb loomed in the center. I remembered the moment in Ketchikan when I had wondered whether I could ever love the mountains again, because of what they had done to Timmy and to me. Now here we were claiming Devil's Thumb as our mountain, always glad when it was part of the view ("Hey, look; there's Devil's Thumb!"), reaching out to make a friend of the enemy, because Timmy's death had sanctified it.

It was now our terrible Holy Mountain.

We had been there, and suffered there, and the goddam mountain was part of us. It had killed our Tim, and harbored him for a time, and yielded him back to us. It had become what the Hindus call an "auspicious" place; a place of power; a damning/saving place. A place to hate. A place to love. Our place, for better or for worse.

That afternoon we went for a swim in a quiet inlet, and took some pictures, and then later I made arrangements for us to go home.

Petersburg is a hard place to get to and a hard place to get out of. There were only a few Air Alaska flights to Seattle, and most of them were booked for the next few days. This was Thursday, and the first clear reservation we could get was for Monday.

Peter made plans to leave on Saturday. He had come out with Rita so that she would not have to be alone. Now that Rains and I were there he had no need to stay. But he now belonged to us in a new way, and we felt that when we waved goodbye to him at the airport.

That evening Rita asked suddenly if I wanted to see Timmy's body. I said no, instinctively. I'm not sure why. I wasn't afraid of dead bodies. I had seen both my grandmothers right after they died. But Tim was so alive for me, I was afraid his dead body might betray his life. I guess I just didn't want to see him dead. I said, "Timmy isn't there anymore."

The next morning Rita got up before the sun and went for a long walk by herself. She decided then that she did want to see his body, so she walked out to the airport, with mist rising over the marshes as the early morning sun gradually warmed the earth. She knew that Charlie Roesel would be at the airport early. She told Charlie that she wanted to see Tim's body.

He apologized that he hadn't done any funeral preparation because he knew that we were going to have him cremated in Seattle. State law says that you have to embalm a body if it is going to be transported across state lines, so he had done that, but that was all.

Tim was there, laid out naked in Charlie's little mortuary, just as he was when they brought him in off the mountain. But if she wanted to visit that was OK and he would see that the door was open and that no one else was around. So she and Charlie went back into town to the mortuary, and when Charlie had everything ready she went in by herself, to see the body of her soul-child.

She came back just as Rains and I were getting ready to go out for another Lumberjack Special. When she told us where she had been, I said, "How was it?" and she said, "He looks wonderful. You should come."

I didn't want to miss anything. Just as I had instinctively said no when she first asked me, it immediately seemed right the minute she said it. I was grateful that she had had the guts to go and then offer that to Rains and me.

After breakfast I sought out the young Presbyterian minister in town. He was short and wiry, bristling with energy, friendly, scholarly and oddly out of place in an Alaskan fishing village. His house was small and very tidy, with bookcases everywhere. His wife was also a theologian, studying at Yale Divinity School, while he carried on alone there in Petersburg. He was excited that I taught in a seminary in Boston. He showed me his books with pride and wanted to talk about Rudolf Bultmann and his de-mythologizing of the New Testament.

84

I didn't want to talk about that.

I asked if he could loan me a robe and a stole. I told him about Tim, and that we were planning a little family service with prayers and anointing. He was sympathetic and glad to help. He and his wife later wrote us a long and sensitive letter about their ministry in Petersburg, and how often bush pilots and fishermen were killed in accidents, and how much aware they were that nature was dangerous in this beautiful place, and that life was precarious.

They came to see us in Wayland after we got home, in a van they had fitted out themselves for camping, and had driven overland from Alaska. He had put together an elaborate tool kit, ready for any emergency. I liked them both, and admired their sense of adventure, and was sorry to hear later that they had been divorced.

The robe he gave me was not one of the black silk academic gowns I wore in Boston, or the thin white cotton cassocks I wore in the Church of South India. This one looked like it had been hand-woven by someone in the church. It was an off-white natural wool material, fairly heavy and rough textured. I didn't want something black or white. Those two absolute, end-limit colors seemed too final. I was glad for something earthy, and in-between, with a little hope left in it. I thanked him for the robe and the green stole he gave me to go with it, and went back to the motel to find Rita and Rains.

We took the car that Gary had loaned us, and parked on the roadside out of town to look for wild flowers. This would be the only time we would see Tim before he was cremated. (Was Rita right? Would it be him, or only the body he had left?)

No one thought to go out and *buy* flowers. We needed

85

something that we had found, and done, and brought; rough and growing; scraggly, but not unlovely. So we found our flowers in huge bunches in the bright August sunshine there on the roadside; goldenrod and fireweed and daisies, and elegant, high, thin grasses to set them off; and we clutched them to ourselves as we rode silently to say goodbye to Tim.

Charlie's mortuary was downstairs from their apartment, which was on a side street in town. It reminded me of those movies of the Old West. There were board sidewalks and some of the buildings had false fronts. The front of the mortuary was plain, and when we walked in it was softly half-lit, the way those places are.

Tim's was the only body laid out. He was off to the left in a better lit corner of the room, naked, with his hands folded over his chest.

Rita was right.

It was Tim.

It wasn't just a body he had left behind.

Is it the Chinese who talk about a moment after death when the spirit finally leaves the body?

He seemed to have waited for us. The body of a nineteen-year-old boy/man in great physical shape is a beautiful thing anyway. He had a fractured skull, a broken neck, and a broken leg, but he didn't look busted up.

It was a shock to touch him, though. I laid my hand on his forehead, and he was cold. That was so strange because I always touched him and held him a lot when he was little, so I knew how his body felt. I used to pick him up by his arms, just above the elbows, and I can still feel those little pipe-cleaner arms in my large hands; feel him wiggle and laugh when I hugged him, and how warm he was in his skinny little way, all ribs and elbows and kneecaps, and hard forehead beneath the mop of hair. And when he got older he was sometimes awkward in his affection, but he always gave me a big hug when we greeted each other. I could feel his hard muscles, and the warmth of his tall, taut body when he hugged me.

Now I touched his forehead, and his skin felt like a sheet of cold plastic, stretched thin over a cement mold. But when I looked at his face he was still there, and it was as though the cold feel of his body was his way of making distance, and saying that we couldn't hug each other anymore, that love was now only *agape,* the pure love of the spirit, and no longer *eros,* the love we feel in our bodies. They say there is no marriage in Heaven, and I guess fathers don't get to hug their sons in Heaven either. That seems so strange, but I didn't want to hug him then. It seemed disrespectful.

Months later, in the first dream I had about Tim, he was really there, like the visions of Old Testament prophets. He came into the bedroom in Wayland when I was sitting on the bed alone, and he was like he was there in Petersburg, unsmiling and distant, but not unfriendly or unkind. He didn't look at me directly. He stood looking out the window, and he didn't say very much, just that he was OK and was glad that we were OK, and that he was now going his own way.

I stood at Timmy's head. Rita was on his right, and Rains on his left. We had murmured to each other when we first came in about how he looked so much himself. We each said hello to him, very quietly, and told him we loved him. Rains had brought Tim's ice-axe. He put the handle in his hands, with the head lying across his chest, and then he really did look like a young warrior on his shield.

I anointed his forehead, and his hands, and his feet, and said a blessing each time. I used some coconut oil

I had brought with me from India for hand lotion. Lots of people in India use it on their hair, and I loved it because the smell was India to me. Then I said a prayer which I had written out. I think it was the truest prayer I ever said, but I don't remember any of it now, and I lost the only copy I had. It is just as well. It was for Tim, and it went with him. Rita read a poem for Tim, and Rains read the poem Timmy had written about how they were bound together in their climbing.

To Rainsford

We have climbed the heights together
and danced in magical air
among crystal towers,
over enchanted granite waves,
plunging our bodies in joyous wonder
into the forbidding peaks of our dreams.
Joined as one,
we have drunk the sparkling water of life,
finding unity in our web
strung high on sweeping walls.
Hanging between sky and earth,
we revel in lofty halls
of mountain majesty
and cleanse our dusty souls
in frozen purity.

After that we wheeled him over to the other side of the room where Charlie had left the casket open, and we lifted his body and laid it in the casket. Tim was almost six feet six inches tall, and he must have weighed about one-hundred-eighty-five normally, but now his body was full of embalming fluid, and it was leaden. I held him with my hand supporting the back of his head.

Under his curly hair I could feel where his skull was fractured, and I laid his head very gently on the pillow of the casket, so I wouldn't hurt him.

Then we gathered up the flowers and put them all around in the casket, and we all laid our hands on him while I said a benediction.

That was all.

We stood at the casket for a while, fussing with the flowers. Nobody cried.

After a while Rita went outside into the sunlight, and I stood in the doorway, watching Rains.

Rains was putting flowers in Timmy's hair.

I remember all the gear laid out on the playroom floor in Wayland, and teasing these macho guys about looking like medieval knights, and how climbing was the moral equivalent of war. And now it was ending with one brother naked and dead, and the other carefully intertwining wild flowers in his curls, like a young girl in love.

Rita wanted to get a picture of Rains and me standing in the doorway, so we did that and then we went out to lunch, and we all said how glad we were that we had gone to see him, and had our service, and how great Tim looked, and how good Charlie had been to us.

Then later Rita and I went for a walk together, and I was suddenly angry. I stopped in the middle of the sidewalk and started out softly, with my voice slowly rising,

"Where is he? Where did he go? I've been good about this. I took everything in stride. I tried to do the right thing, and I'm not blaming anybody, OK? I just want to know where the hell is he?

"Why isn't he here?

"What does he have to do that he can't come home and be with us?"

89

I did not actually call out to him to come back. Later I did that a lot, when I was alone, driving up to New Hampshire from Wayland on winter nights with the sunroof open in the Benz so I could feel the cold, and I would scream to the winter stars for him, and tell him I wanted him to come back, and cry and swear to myself over and over. Then, after a while, I would stop for a cup of coffee and I would be OK.

We still had time before we could leave, so we took the afternoon to go exploring, and watch the salmon go upstream to spawn. The air was clear and the afternoon sun still hot, and the water in the shallow stream was as clear as I've ever seen.

The salmon were committed to this forward move. We watched for a long time, and not one ever turned back. They were going to make it up there or die trying. The water was only four or five inches deep, and the rock barriers to the next highest pool often were a few inches above the water. The salmon would circle and then make a pass for the next jump, and when they missed they would circle and try again, and eventually scrape and slide along to the next pool. You could see the scratches on their bodies where they had banged themselves on earlier rocks.

I'm not sure they were going home, but there was some place they had to get to, and they were giving their all to get there. That effort seemed only curious at first, like the biological riddle of the homing instinct in birds. But the longer I watched, the more moved I was by a commitment which now seemed brave and heroic, not simply instinctive. Had we been choosing up sides for a crucial adventure, I'd pick them for my team. They were really going for it.

And the wonder of going for it in those "great high

90

peaks of the Spirit" kept coming back to me. Freeman Dyson, a friend in Princeton who was a climber in his youth and knows this passion, wrote, "I cannot condemn it, in spite of all the grief it brings." And I realized that I cannot condemn it either. Already I had said, "I can see why those guys wanted to come," and the salmon reconfirmed that. The salmon die after they get upstream and lay their eggs. Nineteen is too young to die, but climbing a mountain is also a great way to go.

If you are going to live, don't hunker down. Fare forward. Do not go gentle. Timmy and the salmon are onto something.

Coming back from Yosemite in the spring of 1976, Tim wrote a poem about how he wanted to live, and how he wanted to die. I quoted it later in a sermon built around Blake's wonderful lines, "Bring me my bow of burning gold/ Bring me my arrows of desire/ Bring me my spear, O Clouds unfold!/ Bring me my chariot of fire."

Sunset from Flight 735

Gazing through a vacuum-sealed window
from this pressurized and regulated world
across a metallic plane of regimented screws,
my heart flies,
dancing out with God
to revel in the wild surging flames
of the dying day.

The blazing torch rejoices,
painting fiery skies
with bold, deep orange strokes

91

and tinting milky peaks
with the smoldering pink of alpenglow.

I want to laugh aloud
as my savage joy strains
against these worldly bonds
and when I die
I only pray that I go down
in such ecstatic glory
as the sun.

Finally it was time to leave Petersburg. We said goodbye to Pat Roesel, and walked out to the airport, while
Gary and Shari Roesel brought our stuff out in Gary's
car. Rita and Rains were coming with me, we had the
body of our precious Tim, and we were going home to
Jonathan and Christina, so my cherished near and dear
were at hand. But the goddam Holy Mountain remained
behind, immobile and unfeeling and everlasting. And
we were leaving Charlie and Pat and Shari and Gary.
We were grateful to them, and wanted to claim them
as friends. And the "auspicious occasion" of Timmy's
Alaska Death was now over. A terrible bond had been
fashioned with Rita and Rains, because we had been
there together. And an emptiness was there between
Jonathan and Christina and me, because they hadn't
been there.

I have often thought back to my stopover in Boston
on the way to Alaska, and my conversation with Jonathan, and how Tina was afraid her daddy was going to
cry. If I had it to do over again I would gather them up
and say, "Hey, let's go to Alaska." But, at the time,
when I asked Jonathan whether or not he wanted to go,
he had said that he needed to be there in Wayland, and
that I should go, and that they would be OK. I was glad

for that because I knew I had to go, and I wasn't sure I could cope with taking them, so I guess it wasn't a very honest question to begin with.

I didn't ask Christina. I didn't treat her seriously enough. She was fourteen, and it must have been hard for her to know what to say or think. She knows now. When I read her part of this story she said, "I wish I had been there." I wish she had, too. I don't think she would have wanted to come, at the time. But it would have made a big difference for us both if I had taken her more seriously, and asked her how she felt. I wish we all had been able to be there together.

Charlie met us at the airport, and he had our tickets all ready, and the documents for Tim's body, along with information about the undertakers in Seattle who would meet the plane and take the body to their crematorium. I checked our bags in the tiny office, and then Rains and I went out onto the tarmac with Charlie to see about loading Tim's body on the plane.

The good weather had finally broken, and the sky was appropriately gloomy and gray, but no hint yet of the oncoming autumn chill. The casket was ready on a dolly and the three of us wheeled it to the cargo bay of the plane, and cranked it up level so that we could slide it into the bay. The baggage guy on the plane gave us thumbs up when it was in and settled, and we stood there under the wing of the plane saying goodbye to Charlie.

In time of trouble, undertakers can be a pain in the ass. I remembered Grandma Rouner's funeral in Brooklyn years before. When we got to the crematorium a short, fat, bald undertaker, smelling hugely of cheap cologne, actually rubbed up against me, like a large black cat, as the Muzak came on, and the side curtain opened dramatically on a fountain playing in the outer garden, and he purred softly, as he had so many times before, "I hope our services will be a comfort to you."

I looked around for an oven to stick him in.

But Charlie, God love him, was not your ordinary undertaker, and he didn't know anything about The American Way of Death. Charlie knew about bush pilots who get killed trying to land in impossible places; and fishermen who fall overboard in the icy cold; and guys who drink too much and smash up their pick-ups; and rich kids from the East who come out to do Devil's Thumb and don't make it.

Charlie is a real human being doing a good job at something nobody else wants to think about. He loved us and we loved him and there was no way to say what he had meant to us, so I just gave him a hug and said, "Thanks, Charlie," and Rains hugged him too, and then we went to get Rita and got on the plane.

It was dark when we landed in Seattle. Rains and I went with the Seattle undertaker to get the casket off the plane and into his limousine. We all rode with him in his elegant car to the funeral home, and then Rains and I got the casket out of the back of the limousine and put it on one of their chrome-plated carts with big, soft rubber wheels, and pushed it silently down a long carpeted walk under an awning into the austere foyer of the building.

It was night and nobody was there. Lights were on only in a few places, so it seemed both brightly lit and dark at the same time. There was some confusion about our schedule, but we finally got that straightened out, and wheeled the coffin into the crematorium. We were leaving for Boston the next day, and crematoriums work twenty-four hours a day, so Rains and I lifted the

94

casket to the appropriate oven, and slid it in, and I closed the door, and said, "Goodbye, Tim," and the funeral guy threw a couple of switches – I thought of Auschwitz – and we looked dumbly at the oven for a moment as it fired up, and then we left.

The only other issue was the urn for the ashes.

Did we want the special-class, super-heavy-duty, expensive urn which would last for a thousand years and protect our loved one appropriately; or did we want the el cheapo urn for people who do not care?

That was the low point of the day, but after he had given us his el cheapo spiel he recovered his humanity. We explained that we were going to bury Tim at High Meadow Farm, and that we only wanted something to keep his ashes in for a few days. Our first thought was a thick coated paper box which they offered for free, but that looked a little shaky, so we opted for the next model, a thin metal box, guaranteed to last for at least a couple of weeks until he was safely part of the good earth in New Hampshire.

The next day we had a direct flight to Boston. I collected the urn from the undertakers, and paid their bill. Rita had a scarf she had knit for Tim that we wrapped the urn in, and I took it to get through security, while Rita and Rains went to get our seats. We were a little late for the flight, and the security people were not ready for us.

The urn looked like a bomb.

I acknowledged that, but I showed them the papers from the funeral home. They wanted me to put the urn through the airport radar. I was incredulous. No way. Timmy is not baggage. "Well, I'm sorry, sir, but you'll have to talk to my supervisor." When he showed up I blistered him.

I was not rational.

If your son dies, you don't have to be rational. Membership has its privileges.

He had two options: he could say OK, or he could call the cops. He said OK.

I got to the gate just as they were closing the doors. They asked nervously about the urn. I ignored them and got on the plane.

Rains held the urn all the way to Boston. I loved how he cherished his brother. Once we had settled in, I started thinking about the services we would have for Tim, and what we needed to do as a family. I thought we should all have rings with Timmy's initials on them, so we could take him with us. I wanted something tangible of Timmy that I could hang on to. I still needed a life raft. A detail. A tangible fact.

Rita and Rains said that they thought that was a good idea, and eventually we did that. When the rings were ready Rita and Rains and Jonathan and Christina and I went to the church in Wellesley where we had had one of the services for Tim. No one else was there, and the church was dark, except for a little pool of light at the altar. I put the rings on the altar, and blessed them the way you do at a wedding, and then we each gave them to each other, there in the dark, starting from Christina to Jonathan, and each said a blessing to the other about remembering Timmy, and believing in life, and loving each other.

IV

Wayland to High Meadow Farm, August 20th–September 1st, 1977

Meanwhile, in Wayland, the rock had arrived. Jonathan took Tina and a couple of friends to get it. At Logan Airport they finally found the air freight building and said that they had come for their package.

"Well, actually, it's a rock."

The freight guy looked at them curiously, said, "I know the one," and led them straight to the crate, balsam sprig and all. Jonathan was cool. He said, "Yeah, that's it, thanks a lot," and signed for it. Nobody laughed till they got it in the trunk of the Benz, and Jonathan started his imitations of the guy's face when he realized that these were the rock people, and everyone laughed and added their own little twists to the story.

Suddenly, they were free.

For a brief and blessed moment everything was lightness of heart, and Jonathan was his funny self again, and a bunch of teenagers were tooling along the turnpike,

The Long Way Home

Jonathan driving like a maniac, with the sunroof open in the sacred Benz, the car Timmy loved and had driven like a maniac himself, having a lark in a world where they didn't have to know about death, and wouldn't have believed in it anyway; where things turn out right; a world full of sunlight, where everybody knows how to take a joke.

That moment must have been special relief for Jonathan, who was now in charge of a growing household. The youngest of three sons, each two years apart, he was always scrambling to keep up with the big boys. But now everyone older was gone, and he was father to a household. Timmy's girlfriend, Ellen, and her sister Lisa had come. Francie, who had lived with us for a year after high school, came from New Orleans with her two-year-old daughter Melanie. And there were friends of our children who lived in Wayland and stopped by constantly to see how everyone was, and what they could do to help, and to be part of the event. Not to mention all the neighbors who called, and sent more food than even a gang of ravenous teenagers could eat.

When I got home I found a list on my desk, in Jonathan's precise handwriting, of everyone who had called, and everyone who had brought anything:

"8/19/77 Anne Walton, casserole;

"8/19 Aunt Betsy called . . ." – and on, and on.

At the high holy times – births, and weddings, and deaths – that's what we want to know. When was he born? What did she wear? How did he die? The rest is mystery. Jonathan kept track of what we could know, and hang on to.

Rains and Timmy were always the gung-ho guys in the dirty blue jeans, who loved loud rock music, smoked pot, and lusted for wild adventure. Jonathan, making his own way, was neat and well organized, a team player

100

who liked institutions and worked well in them. But he was usually the little brother in their growing years, while Rains and Timmy were "the boys."

There was one year, however, when Rains was away at the White Mountain School, and the politics of the family changed. Timmy and "Jay" were now "the boys," and shared the third floor, and got to be buddies. Later, Jonathan wrote a story called "Brothers," which showed how much being a brother meant to him.

But now his parents and his only living brother were far away, and he was responsible. Keeping lists and saying thank you to the neighbors was easy. The hard part was that Rita hadn't had time to tell anyone what had happened, except for her immediate family, and I hadn't been able to tell anyone. Seventeen years old, and Jonathan had to call relatives, and friends, and bear their shock and grief and anger with them, over and over again, as he told them that Timmy was gone. My brother Arthur said later, "You have no idea how gentle and kind Jonathan was when he told us."

And he struggled with his own grief and guilt. He confessed that he felt ashamed because the thought had flashed through his mind that now he could have Timmy's stereo. I said I knew how that was. I confessed that the thought had flashed through my mind that we now had one less college tuition to pay. I told him I knew Timmy would want him to have his stereo, and that he shouldn't feel bad about thinking that.

Jonathan will do many things he can be proud of later in his life, but he'll never do any better thing than he did that week.

We had a lot of mail and I went out to the mailbox every day to get it. Later I was glad for the letters, but at the time I hated the mailbox. It was only about thirty yards from the study, but it seemed like an impossible

101

task to go out there. I felt immobilized, leaden-limbed, unable to summon the motivation for that enormous push out over the lawn, one stagger at a time, like some overloaded beast of burden. And without Timmy in the world, who cared about the mail anyway?

But I was glad for other mindless jobs and I spent several hours one morning washing and cleaning out my car. When I finished, I stood back, admiring and resenting it. There was the Sacred Benz in all its glory, untouched by events, shining and grand, untroubled and unblemished, despite the devastation of those who drove it and loved it.

My father had a Mercedes, and I had wanted one for years. Friends used to kid me about it, and my graduate assistant even gave me a toy one for Christmas one year. Then we had a windfall in 1976, so we got a Wagoneer for Rita, and the Benz for me. Rita gave me a hard time about how expensive it was but I had loved wanting one, and now I loved having it. Jonathan had gone with me to test drive it, once I decided on the five-cylinder diesel. The salesman had tried to sell me a BMW, assuring me that it would "run circles around anything Mercedes makes." I told him that I had three teenage boys, and I didn't want a car that would run circles around anything.

He said, "You're not going to let your kids drive it, are you?" and I said, "Sure, that's part of the point." I remembered how much I had liked driving my father's car, and it gave me a lot of satisfaction to see what a good time they had when Rains and Tim took the car on a climbing expedition, and Tina and her date drove to the Junior Prom, and Jonathan and his girlfriend went off to the movies.

I didn't cry over important things during that week, but I started to cry remembering how much Timmy liked the Benz, and how he wasn't here to see how great it looked. Rita came out of the house and saw me, and didn't need an explanation. She gave me a hug, and then I gathered up my bucket, and the vacuum cleaner, and we went back in the house.

I still have the car, twelve years and 300,000 miles later, and it still looks new. It has cost a lot to keep it up. I can't really afford it, and Rita still gives me a hard time about it, but I like things that last a long time. I still have a couple of sportcoats I wore in prep school, and I'd love to keep that car going till it's twenty years old, or maybe till it hits 500,000 miles. Then, when I can't run it regularly anymore, I'll probably keep it up in the barn, and on special occasions I'll go take a spin in the Benz for Tim.

The house was constantly full of the children's friends, and there was always music playing on the stereo: Crosby, Stills, Nash, and Young; Jefferson Airplane; Van Morrison; James Taylor; rowdies like The Marshall Tucker Band, and lots of others I didn't know. I was struck with how sad so many of those late sixties and early seventies songs are.

Out of all that music we discovered an anthem. It became our Timmy song; our dirge; music to remember him by. When one of us was really bummed we were more than likely to go off and play it. Tina used to do that a lot, by herself, in the room she took over from Timmy on the third floor, crying her heart out. It was a record which Tim had given to Jonathan that year they held forth together on the third floor when Rains was away at school. Jonathan was surprised that it wasn't a loud rock and roll number. Unlike most of Timmy's records, he really liked this one.

It's John Klemmer's "Barefoot Ballet," a lyrical piece

for tenor saxophone, quite repetitive, undulating gracefully, like a sprightly walk down a winding country
road. The tune is simple and spare, almost ascetic. It
doesn't really have a beginning or an end. You think you
have come in in the middle when you first play it, and
at the end you think he forgot to finish, and I liked that.
It seemed hopeful.

We had decided that we would have a service at St.
Andrew's Church in Wellesley, where Rita had been working with Wellesley College students. That would make
it possible for friends in Wayland and Boston to come.
Then we would go to High Meadow Farm and have a
service at the church in Tamworth, also St. Andrew's,
so that our friends from Sandwich and Timmy's climbing buddies could be there. Afterwards we would have
the burial in the little cemetery at the foot of our driveway. Aaron Quimby, who built our house in 1790, is
buried there with his family. There are dozens of these
cemeteries in Sandwich, most of them originally family
plots, and we have expanded ours a little so that Rita
and I can be buried there, too.

We had the urn with Timmy's ashes on the altar,
wrapped in the scarf Rita had made for him. The rock
was propped up behind the urn, with a small jack pine
we'd brought from Petersburg next to it. High school
friends of our kids had gathered wild flowers from the
countryside, and there were masses of them at the front
of the church. The prelude music was Van Morrison's
"Into the Mystic" and the Andante from Beethoven's
Seventh Symphony. After the Scripture lessons Rains
read from the journal he kept at Devil's Thumb while
waiting for the helicopter to come for them; Rita read
some of Timmy's poems; Jonathan read a poem from a
volume on Ansel Adams' photographs called *This is*

the American Earth; then Rita and Tina sang "Amazing Grace," and I had the congregation stand and sing the last verse with them.

I prayed:

> O God of Grace and God of Glory, we open our grateful and grieving hearts to you in thanksgiving for the life of our Timothy.
> For the strength of his body and the keenness of his mind.
> For the riches of his imagination and the awesome tenderness of his spirit.
>
> We cherish dearly remembered times when he cheered us with his wild sense of fun;
> When he helped us with his sensitivity to feeling and his fairness;
> When he challenged us with new ideas and strong convictions;
> When he loved us with that half-shy intensity which bespoke so much integrity.
>
> We give you thanks, O Lord, for all this, and for all those who helped Tim along life's way, and made life such a blessing for him:
> His teachers in school and college.
> His friends in India and here at home.
> His mother, whom he adored,
> His younger brother and sister, whom he cherished,
> His older brother, who was his best friend, and boon companion,
> His larger family of grandparents, uncles, aunts, and cousins, in whose company he delighted.

We give thanks especially for those who taught him to ride, and to ski, and to climb;

Who taught him to love poetry and to think well; and those who taught him the meaning of love.

And we thank you too, Lord, for the beauty of your earth, for all things bright and beautiful, which were an inspiration for Tim, and are a healing balm for us: for rivers, and forests, and those great high peaks of the Spirit which Tim loved so well.

We bless him to your infinite care and goodness, confident that for him, and for us too, "all shall be well, and all manner of thing be well."

We are grateful for all those who have helped us in time of trouble: family and friends who have upheld us, and perhaps especially the good people of Petersburg, Alaska, to whom we were total strangers, but who cared for us because they saw our need.

And finally, O Lord, we pray for ourselves. In your good time heal over the black hole in our hearts, but bless us continually with the memory of Tim's free spirit.

"Born of the sun, he traveled a short while toward the sun," and on his way blessed us beyond measure.

For that great gift, O Lord, we praise your holy name.

Amen.

The prayer wasn't hard to write because it was all thanksgiving, and I wrote it with my heart. But my head still needed to know what an accident is, and what to make of God's power. I had been able to think that God's power in the world is all goodness, because that was all I had known. But now that evil had happened to me, I couldn't accept the idea that this evil is beyond God's reach. And omnipotence has to be part of who God is. The God who sustains and redeems the world is also the God who told the protesting Job to keep suffering. Whatever else that story means, it means that unfair human suffering is somehow encompassed by the power and purpose of God.

Bill Coffin, when he was minister of Riverside Church in New York, lost his son in a car accident, and preached a sermon remembering a woman who tried to comfort him by saying that his son's death was God's will. Coffin said no, that when his son died, God's heart was the first to break.

My friend Jürgen Moltmann, who is a theologian, said something like that when he wrote to me after reading part of this story. "Are you not still 'on the way'? Can one ever get 'home' with such an experience? I don't know either. The old story of Katharina of Siena came to my mind again and again. She cried once to God: 'My God, where were you as my heart was in darkness and the shadow of death?' And she heard the answer: 'My daughter, didn't you feel it? I was in your heart.' This is a mystical answer to the unsolvable metaphysical theodicy question, an answer at least with which one may survive and remain on the long way home, perhaps. . . ."

Because God is a God of love, that's got to be right. But then what saves you from a theology of a Helpless God, because that *can't* be right?

The idea of predestination intended to do that. I don't

believe that God condemns people before they are born, or determines that they will do evil before they choose to. But predestination was a way of explaining how the God who really is God really does rule the whole world, good and bad, and really does save us from the powers of sin and death.

We all die. Some ways are better than others, and Timmy really had a good death. So I only need to know that he really is now in God's care. And I don't mean some abstract idea of how he is remembered in the mind of God forever, and that that is immortality, because it isn't. I mean that the real Tim really is in the ever-loving care of the real God, the One who is closer to us than we are to ourselves, and has the whole world in his hand. Or, as Julian of Norwich put it, "That all shall be well, and all manner of thing be well."

I take new comfort from knowing that God's rain falls on the just and the unjust, and God's sun shines on the evil and the good. Timmy's death was not fair. That was *really* Bad News; but if God is not Lord of the Bad News as well as the Good, then he has no more power than our best human yearning for the Good. What I know about God's power is that he turned my mourning into thanksgiving; and in the life of the world to come, I believe he turns death into eternal life. I'm not quite sure what that means, but the power of an omnipotent God to save the world is a belief I cling to.

My theology was helped a lot by letters from friends like Jürgen, especially one from Dan Berrigan. I kept thinking that in Puritan New England people were always losing children, sometimes several; and now in a world of holocaust and genocide I felt ashamed to be so bereft for so long, over the death of a child. But Dan wrote several years after Timmy died:

Please give my warmest to Rains. I had known nothing of Tim's death and am sorrowing with you and your family. We lost John Leary in Boston a year ago, and David Joyce here on Good Friday.

Grief goes with our days—and perhaps is a holy link with such horrors in the world as might find us otherwise hard of heart.

Christ comforts us all,

Daniel

But I do believe in accidents, because I trust that God gives us freedom, and accidents, or mistakes, are the price of freedom.

I don't know what happened to Tim. I still think the snow must have balled up in his crampons, and he lost his footing, and fell over backwards, and skidded in the wrong direction. I don't blame God for that, or Timmy either. He knew the risks, and so did I.

I blame myself for not knowing where they were, and not paying enough attention to Tim, but not for the fact that they wanted to do that climb, and not for failing to tell them not to do it. Freeman Dyson told me that he took crazy risks climbing when he was a teenager. He had climbed college buildings at Winchester and Cambridge in England, in the dark, without helmet or rope. After a rock climb in Wales, where another climber had died, and he himself had been injured, he wrote that he "came home in a state of shock, and my mother seized the opportunity to extort a promise that I would do no more climbing, either buildings or mountains, for at least a year. That promise saved me. I climbed again in later years, but never with that reckless adolescent passion."

109

Rains was always the one with "that reckless adolescent passion" and when he confessed that he had done similar "solo" climbs, without protection, I made him promise he would never do that again. I very seldom asked any of the kids to promise anything like that. I probably should have done more.

Later, the question about the nature of accidents was raised by a couple Rita and I went to for marriage counseling. I'm told that the divorce rate for couples who have lost a child is very high, and I can believe it. Timmy's death magnified many of our conflicts. This couple believed that there is a psychological explanation for all human actions, and therefore there are no "accidents." They suggested that Timmy's death might be an unconscious suicide, in response to conflict between his parents. They asked me how I felt about that idea.

I was frightened.

I'm intimidated by psychiatrists, and my instinctive reaction was that they must be right, and that I was therefore significantly responsible for Tim's unconscious suicide.

This idea had never occurred to me, and I felt blindsided again, this time by guilt, as well as grief.

That evening I called a psychologist friend and asked him what he thought about that idea. He explained about the "no accidents" school of thought, but said he did not agree with it. Knowing something of our family he said that he didn't think that Timmy's death was suicide. That assurance helped me realize how angry I was, not so much because it was an accusation of me, although I was stung by that, but that it belied Tim's understanding of himself as a climber.

He had written in his journal about his need to find a woman he could love, and the importance of poetry and climbing:

110

Poetry is, I believe, another expression of this desire for beauty and oneness especially when the poems are about a woman and they often are the spark that drives one into poetry. It is an intensity of awareness and involving desire in life and even when it is painful with unfulfilled desires it is better than a shallowness of feeling. However, living from moment to moment in the experience is of major importance, to be heightened by desire, and therefore, I feel that I must find an active way to express this love, for I cannot totally live on a dream.

Climbing is for me this type of experience and intense awareness of life. Here I find joy in the unity of mind and body with the wilderness in the same way that I get happiness out of relations with a woman.

Death-defying adventures are mysterious, and there are lots of levels of meaning in this desire to be melded into a woman and a world; but a theory about suicide is definitive. So this couple was suggesting that he was not really cleansing his "dusty soul in frozen purity," or finding an active way to express love, but killing himself because of the struggle between his parents.

I told Rita that I would not pay to see them anymore.

I wrote them a carefully phrased letter saying that if, as they had urged, they felt a need to work through my feelings on this issue with me, they were welcome to come to my office, but that I would no longer pay them, or come to them.

They did not reply.

Those therapy sessions had been a lifeline for Rita, and she was angry and upset when I refused to go back.

That weekend I drove alone to High Meadow Farm, and went down to the cemetery and cried out for Tim so loudly I was afraid the neighbors would hear, half a mile away. I rubbed my Timmy ring back and forth over the rock, to gouge something of his into something of mine, and went back up to the house and cried most of the afternoon.

High Meadow Farm is an archive of our family history, from Indian carpets and paintings and old family photographs, to the new barn we built when the children first had horses. I relived much of our history that afternoon. I wandered past the wallpaper Rita had put up; admired again her genius for mixing paint colors; remembered how much the children loved the swing we hung between the box stalls in the barn, and how Rita labored over the nursery, preparing for Jonathan's birth.

But the children and I all had "other things to do," and she was hurt by that. I knew it, and went to the study and wrote this poem:

Homeless

For a brief time I was safe
In a quiet room.
My parents were always there.
I trusted them to help and to
Defend me from the
Other one, my precious bane of the strong body and
The stinging tongue.
He of the singing spirit and
The freezing will.

I have inhabited other rooms, in other places.
I have drained drops of burnt umber from my
Dark heart's blood to make barn red deep.

The Long Way Home

I have chipped flakes of blue from my eyes
With exquisite care to lend sky's poignance to
Our dining room; pasted paper with love's juices to
Festoon nurseries, and welcome the new born.
I have crafted world-womb cradles for my loves,
Offering the still deep of
My inner ocean, tranquil and clear, to mirror fern
And wind-bent bough for them.

But they would not stay.
They loved other places, other rooms.
Or cherished places I had left.
Barn red is only paint without the stamp of horses,
The squeals of children swinging,
The glow of life together.
He went to India, or the study,
Proud of my paint and papering,
But clutching his passport to an alien world.

They went to Harvard, or to practice, or wherever.
I did not want to hold them back.
I wanted to go with them; not to Harvard, or to
    practice,
Or to India,
But on their inner journey.
Oh, do not freeze me out, or scorn me!
I have no gift for stoic strengths.
I am not ice, or steel, or even Reason.
My strength is willow's wind-bent bough,
And I can show you grace in places
You rush by.

I call to them; they do not hear me.
My spirit-child, soul-mate, heard
But he is gone forever, and I am hurt

113

Beyond repair, to have my dream so shattered,
My companion dead.

So I came to this quiet room, willow-weak and
    willow-strong,
Hope dimmed, but hoping still
To be companioned,
To be nurtured, so that I can nurture,
To scratch my willow branch against the frozen pane
Of his mercurial heart,
And have him open to my dancing in the Spring
    wind.

Perhaps we were not truly with each other,
There in that quiet room,
He paternal, I wary.
Still, it was safe.
World womb offering is a treasure
No one gifted me.
I know these folk were not my parents,
This quiet room no womb world.
Still, I am not greedy.
I have learned to live on scraps,
And I was fed.

But now his icy reason, his Philosophy,
Has forged forceps of his will,
And I am untimely ripped
From even this poor womb scrap.
Barn red without soul's umber is but paint,
And I am mocked by talk which promised care
Yet tore me from my solace.

Again the beast prowls my dark,
Sharp tongued banshees scream their ridicule,

114

I freeze with fear,
And am again forsaken.

Only later did I realize that I had dealt with my pain by imagining hers. I was glad for that empathy, but it was also an escape from myself. I had not yet learned to claim my own story.

A day or so after the service in Wellesley we all migrated north and had several days at High Meadow Farm before the service there.

That was a strangely happy time.

We were surrounded by kids. Tina's special high school friends from Wayland, Rains' roommates and friends from Harvard, Timmy's roommate and friends from Hampshire, friends from Sandwich, and lots of others. Having lost a precious child, all these other precious children rushed to comfort and celebrate us. While they were in Wayland they had all developed a running gag about "Coneheads," which I never entirely got. I think I missed out on the relevant TV program, but it seemed to have something to do with those orange plastic cone highway markers.

Never mind, they were all the Cone Family, and there was regular high hilarity regarding the latest Cone joke. Then Chip Lee, Tim's climbing buddy from Hampshire, asked what he could do to help, and we sent him down to the pond to scrub the rock steps, thus initiating the Chip Lee Memorial Scrubbing Brush, which became a new joke. And so it went.

With all the climbers around it was inevitable that new routes would be charted on the house and barn, and "Barn Wall Direct" became the major challenge for the experts. Here I must confess the total admiration of a little kid for big boys who do miracles. The finger

115

holds are about seven feet off the ground, and exactly three-eighths of an inch wide. Rains and Tim used to chin themselves from their fingertips repeatedly on that tiny grip, and now the other hot-shot climbers were doing the same. I stood there laughing in amazement, delight, and unabashed admiration.

The kids set up the stereo out on the driveway between the house and the barn. They also made a rustic shrine, with the urn, still wrapped in the scarf Rita had made, placed carefully on top of Timmy's Everest, a very large boulder about a hundred yards above the barn. It got its name in 1961 when Timmy was three, and Rita explained to him that we were going to India where there was Mt. Everest, the biggest mountain in the world. Later, on a walk in what was then dense woods, they came upon this very large boulder, and Timmy asked, "Is that Mt. Everest?"

The kids would dance out in the driveway to the latest rock hits, and wander down to the pond for a skinny-dip, and then go up and sit by Timmy's Everest and have a beer and talk about Tim and about themselves. It was a sad time, and they cried a lot, but it was never somber, and little Melanie ran around happily and gave us all a sense of new life. Every funeral needs a two-year-old.

The service in Tamworth was a repeat of the one we had done in Wellesley, except that my brother Arthur, his daughter Kristen, and our friend Brian Kelley all took part. The church was jammed, and I was touched by that. I especially remember Willie Kalinuk standing in the doorway, and the grief in his face. Willie ran the Ski School at Mt. Whittier, and taught the boys to ski. He was in his late twenties, skied with the elegance of poetry in motion, and liked kids so much he would collect a gang of them on the mountain after lunch and say, "C'mon, let's go skiing!" and they would all whoop and holler and go hot-dogging after their Pied Piper hero.

Rains and Timmy stayed with Willie and Linda a couple of times on winter weekends after we moved to Wayland, and later, when Mt. Whittier was no longer operating, they would sometimes call Willie and go to Wildcat or Cannon for a day of skiing together.

After the service Willie came to me, tears streaming down his face, punching his fist into his hand, saying "Goddam!" over and over. That was all; but that curse blessed me, perhaps because it was so real. Later my friend and colleague Marx Wartofsky said, "I heard your news, and I just want to say, 'Shit!'"

I loved him for that.

I learned afterwards that his only son had been killed by a car when he was six.

Marx knew.

Christina bravely participated in both the responsibilities and the fun, even though the others were all mostly older and had been a part of Timmy's world which she did not know.

She had been a beautiful child, was becoming a beautiful woman, and had always been a cherished little sister. When Rita was pregnant in India the three boys all hoped loudly for a little sister, so she had been much celebrated since before she was born.

The kind of attention pretty little girls get is often self-serving, but Tina remembered Tim as one who came home, sat her down, and asked her directly about herself. He really wanted to know about her life. He gave her real attention. So Timmy's loss for her, and for us all, is not just the emptiness of his being gone. It is also the positive loss of what he would have been for us now.

Families construct delicate balances, and specific roles. Lose anyone and you unbalance everyone.

Rains needed Tim for his graceful, how-to-take-a-joke lightness of heart, his intellectual companionship, and his sense of life as an open possibility. He could have helped bear some of that heavy weight that inevitably burdens the oldest child and first son of minister/missionary/professors. Timmy's death has doubled that burden, rather than relieved it. Given his sense of responsibility, Rains' life has been virtually absorbed by Tim's death. He needs Timmy to take him out for a beer and say, "For Chrissake, Rains, lighten up!"

Jonathan needed him for companionship, too, but especially for perspective on their very different worlds. Tim had a gift for claiming his own ventures and values without knocking other people's, and he would have been there with Jonathan in his world, even while he was providing him with a window on a different one.

Christina needed Tim for his attention. Building her self-confidence was hard for her, and it was the kind of attention Timmy had given her that helped her most. I'm angry that he wasn't able to be there for her when she needed him.

I still see her in my mind's eye, running down the driveway and screaming when Jonathan told her that Timmy was gone. Even then she didn't know how much she had lost. During the services and Timmy's burial she was brave and present, but she was always the little sister who had been left out of something, as though the others knew a Timmy that she didn't know. Part of her recently regained self-confidence has been claiming the Timmy she did know, and who she knew had really known her.

Rita claimed Tim as her soul child, and did it very gracefully. That was never a problem for anyone while he was alive. His death, however, was like a secret solution washing over her life text, revealing previously invisible ink where something significant was now writ large. I think it would have been easier for her to claim herself if Tim had lived to go his own independent way. He was a model for her, and his venture in growing up would probably have made it easier for her to grow out of her role as mother and into her more independent life and work.

But that didn't happen, and I was jealous of Rita's Tim.

I wanted to be the man she yearned for.

I thought it was wonderful that he envied me for the woman I married, but I was jealous that my wife had such intimacy with another man. In Petersburg, when I wanted to be melded, I knew that that wasn't possible, but I wanted someone who was going to be on my side, and want me, and it was a long time before I felt that from Rita.

I needed him because the Preacher's Kid From Portsmouth, who thought he was perfect, turned out to be something of a rowdy who did bad things. Timmy was a rowdy, too, so I always felt he knew me.

He once took me to a bar in North Conway to have shots of Tequila. Tim had the ritual down pat. They brought the drinks, and we put a rim of salt on the circle made from touching our index finger to our thumb, and then licked off the salt and swigged the Tequila.

Philosophical insights are supposed to come in more dignified circumstances, but I now discover that my creativity is a friend of my previously undiscovered rowdiness. That doesn't equate Tequila with creativity, but I yearn for another night on the town with the irrepressible Tim, to talk about creativity, and how one learns to do one's thing. I think especially of a book I had been working on for years which Tim took an interest in. Others in the family knew I was working on it. Timmy wanted to talk about it, and was the only one who actually read it.

We planned to have the burial following the service in Tamworth, but we didn't have the energy for that, so we had a reception at the house instead, and did the burial a few days later. I remember my father, standing in the receiving line with my mother, like some neighbor or family friend, bereft and inarticulate, not knowing what to do. I guess I wanted him to break through the line, give me a hug, tell me it was OK, cry with me, be a father; I don't know what I wanted. He loved Tim, and was proud of him. He was really struck down. My mother had lost her little brother when he was just a child, so she knew about these things. But Dad believed only the good, and his life was fulfilled by being the patriarch, so he didn't know what to make of this bad thing.

And I know that he felt left out of Timmy's death, because my sister Betsy told me that he had talked to her about it. When he called our house some strange kid would answer the phone, and he'd have to leave a message. I didn't always call back, and he was hurt by that. And even when he finally got to talk with me it seemed to him that Timmy had become a cult figure for me, my family, and this gang of strangers who had gathered around us. He felt like an outsider, and I think my brother and sisters felt excluded, too. Dad didn't like the idea of having the service in an Episcopal church, for fear it would be too stiff and formal. Then when the service was over he felt that it had been too disorganized, too long for such a hot day, and not really Christian enough.

120

I had no energy for him at the time. He and I were both devastated. He was never really there for me, and I missed him. I could have used a hug from my father.

We buried our Tim on Thursday, September 1st, in the afternoon. It was one of those perfect September days characteristic of late summer in New Hampshire. Endless blue sky; clear, sharp air; a few lazy, puffy clouds; hot sun; mid-eighties. There were only about a dozen of us, just family and a few close friends.

This was the end.

Our last ceremonial occasion.

We discovered that we were all good at this. After the first service in Wellesley people had told us how wonderful it was to see the family all there, how strong we had been, what a vivid picture of Timmy we had given them all. And I wanted it to go on forever and hang on to Timmy by celebrating him over and over. As long as we were doing this we had him with us. Once he was buried, he was gone. But we knew that we had to do it sooner or later. And now was the time.

We had worked hard in the cemetery for several days, digging the place to set the famous rock, placing it carefully facing west, toward "the great high peaks of the Spirit," and then digging the small grave for the urn right in front of it. Rains had done most of the digging, sweat pouring off him, desperate in his need to do something, despairing in the thought that nothing really mattered any more.

Timmy loved to go barefoot, even in the winter, and we all went barefoot up beyond the barn to Timmy's Everest, to get the urn. The meadow beyond was one he and Bud had cleared, the summer he was sixteen, to open up a view of Mt. Chocorua. From the novel about Chocorua, *Look to the Mountain,* by Ellen's grandfather,

121

I rephrased the great Psalm, "I will look to the Mountain, from whence cometh my help. My help cometh from the Lord, who made Heaven and Earth."

Then we all walked slowly down to the cemetery, to the music of "Barefoot Ballet."

Rains carried his brother's ashes, wearing only his shorts. He was as close to naked as he could be, and he had put wild flowers in his hair.

I wore my white cassock from the Church of South India, and we all gathered around the grave. I read the committal service from the Church of South India Prayer Book.

Rita did the burial.

She knelt in front of the rock, placed the urn very carefully in the hole the boys had dug, and said softly, "Goodbye, Timothy."

Then everyone put a handful of dirt on the grave. I said a benediction, we all stood quietly for a moment, and it was over.

Rita, Rains, Jonathan, Tina, and I all started back up to the house together, while the others hung back to let us go.

We were part way up the driveway when we all turned instinctively to hug each other.

We stood there for a long time.

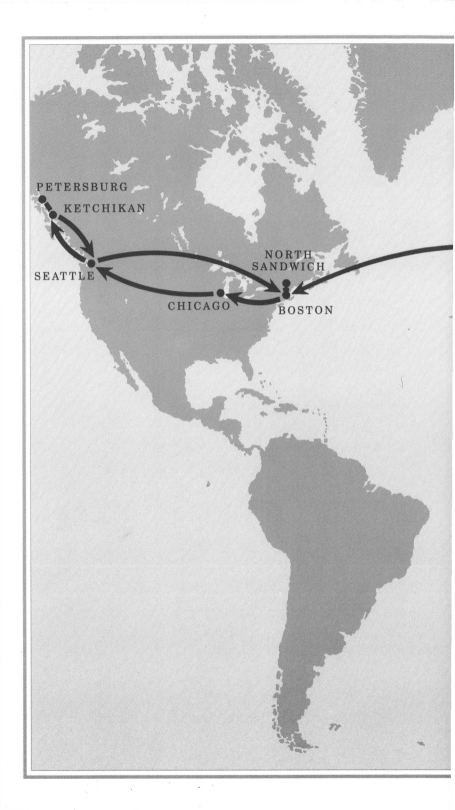